While the Code Compiles
Unusually hilarious tales from IT

Unus T E & Sreekanth S S

First published in India 2015 by Frog Books
An imprint of Leadstart Publishing Pvt Ltd
1 Level, Trade Centre
Bandra Kurla Complex
Bandra (East) Mumbai 400 051 India
Telephone: +91-22-40700804
Fax: +91-22-40700800
Email: info@leadstartcorp.com
www.leadstartcorp.com / www.frogbooks.net

Sales Office:
Unit No.25/26, Building No.A/1,
Near Wadala RTO,
Wadala (East), Mumbai – 400037 India
Phone: +91 22 24046887

US Office:
Axis Corp, 7845 E Oakbrook Circle
Madison, WI 53717 USA

ISBN 978-93-52013-35-7

Book Editor: Surojit Mohan Gupta
Design Editor: Mishta Roy
Layout: Chandravadan R. Shiroorkar

Typeset in Book Antiqua
Printed at Dhote Offset Technokrafts Pvt. Ltd., Mumbai

Price — India: Rs 150; Elsewhere: US $6

Dedication

About the Author

Sreekanth Sasidharan

Sreekanth Sasidharan has 16+ years of experience in the IT industry and has performed different roles from Software Engineer to a Technology Practice Lead. He has done his B. Tech. from CET, Kerala and then his MBA from IIM Bangalore. He continues working in Infosys where he had spent his whole IT career so far. He lives in Bangalore with this family. This is his first book.

Sreekanth - sreekanthss@gmail.com

About the Author

Unus Ebrahim

Unus Ebrahim is an IT professional with 17+ years of experience. He has worked with multiple IT firms namely Infosys, Capgemini, Wipro and Accenture. He has done his B. Tech. from Mar Athanasius College of Engineering, Kothamangalam, Kerala and MBA from IIM Bangalore. He lives in Bangalore with his family. This is his first book as well.

Unus - unuste37@gmail.com

Acknowledgements

This book is inspired by the lighter moments we came across in our long IT careers. Every person we met and every incident we witnessed throughout our working years in the world famous IT firms have contributed to the shaping up of this book. Thanks a ton to all those friends and characters in our IT life who had contributed/lived many of the moments described in this book.

We thank Leadstart Publishing for accepting our first book and agreeing to publish the same. Thank you Malini for promptly replying to all the queries we had regarding the publishing and helping us get this to the readers.

We thank our Editor Mr Surojit Mohan Gupta for guiding us in making our writing better.

We thank our families who stood by us during the creation of this book — when the long hours in the office were followed by a few more long hours at home, working on our dream project — the completion of this book.

We owe much to all of you, who have decided to pick a copy of this book. After all, the ultimate goal of any writer is to reach the readers.

The Story Starts Right Here...

After completing our MBAs from one of the leading IIMs, like any aspiring MBA graduate, we also had this immense feeling to 'change the world with our own global corporation'. Even after thoroughly evaluating several ideas of entrepreneurship such as 'Importing sand from Sahara desert for the Bangalore construction industry' and 'setting up a rehabilitation centre for the 15+ Year IT Managers who have lost 50% of their eye capacity, 30% of the ear capacity and almost 70% of brain capacity', we were nowhere near taking that final plunge.

Several hours and night-outs were spent in making PPTs and applying all the frameworks we learned in MBA to these entrepreneurial ideas. Nothing looked strategically optimal in MBA terms. If the market analysis looked attractive, then the local skill availability wasn't good. If both market and skill projections were good then the operations would look un-scalable. Once the above three were found OK, the break even period appeared too long. After several 'litres' of midnight oil, roadside omelettes and concentrated coffees, we found the answer to the question why all MBA grads work for firms which were started by others. Answer is simple—it's easy to apply the MBA theories and frameworks when someone else is paying you.

Writing a book was the next idea we thought about. Almost every IIM graduate is now jumping into the book writing bandwagon as soon as they get their IIM certificates. So unlike 'real entrepreneurship', that must be something even MBAs from IIMs can do, we thought. But then came the next hurdle, what will we write? We went back to our drawing boards. Like typical management consultants, we drew several 2 X 2 matrices and found that humour and short story quadrant were the most promising ones.

Next few weeks were spent in creating the right plot, which again went to a deadlock. As we were almost on the brink of throwing away the book idea, another thought came up—why not create an imaginary IT campus—the environment of which is very familiar to both of us.

We could not create a real IT campus as we originally planned after MBA. So, an imaginary one will at least partially fulfil our entrepreneurial dreams!

Now, the focus was on building that IT campus of our imagination. The one IT campus which is the epitome of all IT stereotypes. The one which will make you laugh and relax, and not worry about the numerous deadlines in your busy life.

Our main protagonist, the IT company which we christened Infopro, was born and brought up in Bangalore just like many of its more famous counterparts. This IT campus will expose to you the lighter side of IT.

So Dear Readers, lets welcome you to take a 'golf cart tour' of the world famous Infopro campus. You will meet many of the glorified Infoproites in this tour. As you will see in this book, everyone is a hero in Infopro. Every software engineer, project manager, group manager and even the canteen waiters have a story to tell. As you take your tour through the Infopro campus, we will narrate to you interesting stories of a few Infoproites. We have even allowed some of the great storytellers in Infopro to directly narrate their story to you. In either case, we guarantee you that you will enjoy each of those stories and your campus walkthrough will be fun filled and fulfilling.

In software industry, compiling the code usually is a time consuming process. It can take anywhere from several minutes to hours depending on your system. The usual practice is that a coder takes a break while the code compiles. We call such a break, the 'period of good hope' as we hope for the best post the code is compiled. For the lack of a better title and dedicating it to the 'period of good hope', we named this book 'While the code compiles'.

With the hope that you are holding a legitimate copy of the book (and not the one you bought from one of the footpath sellers or a pirated softcopy from the internet), we wish you a very pleasant reading experience.

Sreekanth Sasidharan & Unus Ebrahim

Prologue...

Madhu, the PM in Infopro, was offering his advice to the Unorthodox entrepreneur—Bhikhari Shambhu. "You know what—IT industry and begging industry are similar in many ways. Revenues in both cases are dependent on the number of employees. Your industry has beggars at the ground level. In IT industry, these beggars (rather buggers) sit at every level. In both cases, people management and motivating them for high productivity is important."

"You need to have a HR person to devise policies and track productivity improvements of your people. Recruit someone from IT as both industries are similar," Madhu continued.

"But Sir, will someone leave IT and join my company?" Shambhu was doubtful.

"Of course. Why not? You don't know the guys in IT. You just need to offer 50 paise more than what they get now. They will join for sure. Also, the other thing they look for is 'better' position. If he is a consultant, take him in as a senior consultant. If he is a sweeper, just take him in as a senior sweeper. They will join the next day."

"Is that right ... sir...? I thought these IT people are ... you know, very sophisticated and complex people," Shambhu told frankly.

"Darwin did not mention it in his Theory of Evolution—but actually these IT people are the simplest of the mammals. If you offer grass and water to a cow, it will come with you. Similarly, just offer 50 paise more and a 'senior' role to an IT guy … he will join you… It is so simple."

"Is it…?" Shambhu was enlightened to the core. The image of an IT engineer completely changed in his mind.

"Remember, these beggars employed in your firm are your biggest asset. You should know that every morning, the biggest assets of your company walk out of their huts to the different junctions of Bangalore. They should be treated well."

1: IT Quality Audits — A Survivor's Guide

October–November of every year is known for festivity in Silicon Valley of India, Bangalore. Lot of seasonal goodies arrive during that period. For the IT people, another seasonal guest comes during the period — the Quality Audit.

Nobody knows why exactly quality departments exist in IT companies, but they do exist. Why mosquitoes and houseflies live in our house — no one knows but they do exist. Every October–November they wake up to conduct the internal audits and external audits. As usual, this year also the "Audit Season" arrived and, along with other IT companies, Infopro also joined the audit festivities. Usually the chronological order is: Ganesha festival comes first, then the audit festival and the season ends with the Diwali festival.

Quality folks are like migrating birds. During the audit season, you see a lot of them. You will see them in every nook and corner of Infopro. You will see them in ones, twos and even in large groups. They will be running from one building to another to reach in time for a project review, or sometimes you see them shouting at a project manager for not following the simple 108 point checklist given by them for each project.

Sujay, my Project Manager, came on Monday morning with the shocking news that our project as usual was selected for quality audit this year. Last 3 weeks he was going to the nearby Ganesha temple not only because it was the festival season but also to make sure the "random selection algorithm" misses our project. Ganesha didn't pay attention to his prayers. Actually, all the project managers in the unit were visiting the same temple. So Ganesha decided to be neutral. Sujay charged the cost of all the coconuts he cracked at the temple against the project party fund which was donated by all of us individually.

I was the DP—Defect Prime—of the project (what a name, there is a prime for defects also). Hearing this news, I first thought I would take 2 weeks leave. But, the fact that my leaves for the year had been exhausted and there was no way Sujay would leave me, I resisted that thought. As expected, soon the Quality department folks sent a series of mails. Sample of few mail series are as below:

Tuesday 10:00 AM–11:00 AM: Quality Awareness Session for project team

Wednesday 2:00 PM–3:30 PM: Weekly Project Quality Review (Recurring till external audit is over)

Thursday 2:00 PM–3:30 PM: DP review

Friday 2:00 PM–3:30 PM: Project Risk Review

Friday 4:00 PM to 5:00 PM: Overall review to see if all the above reviews have gone well.

Quality department had already started their "Navarathri programs."

On Tuesday morning, the awareness session started. At 10:00 AM, only the quality guy was there in the room. At 10:06 AM, the freshers joined. The 2-7 yr experienced folks joined by 10:15 AM. And the senior citizens joined by 10:25 AM. Project Manager joined just before the session was over.

Quality Manager for our project, Naveen, started with introduction of quality standards and levels. Though it was morning 11:00 AM, the team started sleeping. The people who were not sleeping were playing games on mobile. One of our team members Sanju even snored. The game players cursed Sanju as they could not concentrate on their games properly. The instructor did not mind as all of his classes had at least 3 or 4 snorers. He was now used to it. He was happy that there was only 1 snorer in this class. Luckily by the time someone's mobile rang and Sanju woke up. Naveen started some interactive Q&A after some time. The main targets were few of the fresh joinees.

Naveen: "Folks do you know why we do quality audit?"

I wanted to answer — 'they do it as they don't have any other job.'

By the time one of the freshers answered "To check the quality level of the project."

Naveen asked the next question, "What level is our project currently?"

Freshers thought it was better to say level 1 as numero uno was the goal which the PM told when they joined the project. So they told first level…

With that Naveen understood the "level" of quality awareness in the project and he did another one hour of lecture on the quality levels and the definitions, etc.

After the meeting, Sujay asked me to do an internal assessment of the project and submit an "FIR" immediately.

I found that after the last November Audit, the project was pretty-much running without any quality activities, just like any other project in Infopro. There were no quality documents being made or updated in the last one year. Since our project was a telecom project, it involved a lab as well. The condition of the lab was pathetic. The wiring inside the lab was running like "festival season" decorations from one corner to another. Many of the wires inside the lab resembled GOD for their other end could not be traced at all.

So I submitted the FIR to Sujay saying the condition was pathetic and in this state even if an internal audit happened, the project would be assessed at level 1 straight and both of us would lose the job. I even suspected that they may rate us at minus 1 or minus 2. Since both of us were job fearing even more than God fearing, we decided to do some 'disaster recovery' of the situation.

We decided to come up with the following actions:

1.   Make all the documents from scratch using "Reverse engineering methodology". Usually you collect the defects, classify them, use the defect prevention methodology to find the root-cause and then attack the root-cause.

Since all the above is a six month process and cannot be done in a natural way now, we decided to first arrive at the root-causes, which we decided were "lack of training", "lot of new engineers joining", etc. According to the above we classified the defects and made the defect data as well.

2.   The supporting XL sheets, word documents, etc., needed to be made. We thought of taking the help of "script specialist" Aravind to make those.

3.   The physical intensive job of lab cleaning was given to the two fresh joinees.

Soon the prep work started. First day when Aravind ran the script, the entire project management tool hung. Ultimately we called the Network and Technology support group (NAT support group which we fondly call NOT Support group because of their past performance and excellent support SLAs). By 6:00 PM, NAT group put our ticket back as 'need more info', as usual, and they left for home. Finally with two days of back and forth status change exercises NAT came and looked at the issue. They found that someone had been trying to extract one year's data at one-shot and that's why the system had hung. NAT rebooted the system to recover it. Aravind later broke his script into 12 pieces and extracted the data month by month.

The lab cleaning was even more eventful. Because of the excessive dust, after the first day, both freshers fell sick. One of them was allergic to dust and developed a chronic asthma. Finally he got a doctor's certificate and escaped from this exercise. Instead, another stronger fresher was posted inside the lab. Also, it was decided that we should be first doing a dust cleanup before doing wire clean-up. The facilities department was contacted. The facilities ladies soon found a few rat families and several bunch of cockroaches from the lab. The discovery of the rat family explained why sometimes mysteriously connections got broken in the lab. So, with one more root cause found, I updated my Defect Analysis Sheet accordingly. Sujay wanted to call Discovery channel. I said Animal Planet would be a better option. Later we ditched it, as we could not decide which channel.

Hearing the news of the rats and cockroaches, the lady team members declared that they would never enter the lab again. The next day, one of the freshers mistakenly pulled out the main power wire from the complete mess of wires and the whole lab went down for 4 hours. Another day one of the freshers found an unused power point and plugged his mobile charger there. That was a faulty power point and the charger burnt, the fire alarm went off, and the whole building was evacuated to debug the situation.

After the lab had been cleaned to a decent level, it was discovered that there was no sign board for the lab. So it was decided to make one. Lot of names got suggested, but finally the name Advanced Network and User Interface System (ANUIS) testing lab was accepted as it had all the right terms like advanced, system, etc. The name was given to the facilities department folks to make a board. Since the name was long, the facilities department decided to put the abbreviation instead so that they could save some money on the size of the board. The illiterate painter, who painted the board, missed the letter 'I' in the abbreviation and the board got made. Upon fixing the board, there was a huge crowd in front of the lab to see what testing was happening. The board just said ANUS lab. Someone asked if the same lab was being used for both men and women. When I said yes, he took me to a corner and said he would like to join the project. He is good with 'both' it seems. I did not understand, so I ignored him.

Several people took the photograph of the board and it also appeared in the *Times of India*'s interesting board feature later. By that time Sujay came and threw the board out.

Aravind somehow created the data. There where holes in the data but at least it was something to start with. The quality team audited the project and raised NCRs. The number of NCRs was so large that it seemed with this data even next year also the project wouldn't pass the audit. Also, the quality team warned that this time a new set of external auditors was coming and hence they were likely to be very neutral and even the quality department wouldn't be able to put pressure on them.

Seeing the situation, Sujay and I decided to undertake some other smart moves to pass the audit.

Accordingly, we decided to find the whereabouts of the external auditor and tried to see whether we could impress him by some other methods. Sujay did some research and found out from the quality department who would be the potential external auditor for our project. He also reached out to his friends in other companies and gathered some intelligence on the 'weaknesses' of the auditor so that we could make some arrangements to appeal to the weak points in order to impress the auditor.

Sujay's investigation revealed that the auditor was from West Bengal and hence we deduced that he would be definitely a fish fan. So, we decided to take him to 'The Harbor', a fish specialty restaurant near Infopro before the audit. Also, Sujay learnt that the auditor would be particularly interested in estimation, so even if other audit items were not well handled and only if the estimation part was taken care of, the audit would pass.

Based on the above inputs, we made the agenda for the audit as below:

1:00 PM–2:00 PM Lunch with the auditor

2:00 PM–3:00 PM Estimation model

3:00 PM–3:30 PM Other audits and lab audit

Finally, the day of the audit arrived.

As expected, the quality folks took the auditor to our building in a golf cart... Naveen called me and Sujay to the side and told:

"*Arey yaar*, the Auditor got changed at the last minute. This is Mr Srinivasan from Chennai."

We felt as if we were part of the Indian football team who were prepared to face Nepal but were suddenly put in front of Germany.

We shook hands with the Auditor. He didn't seem to be particularly impressed by anything and didn't show any emotions. Looks like he was the person who used to stand in Marina beach as the subject of 'Who can make me Laugh' contest.

We took him to the restaurant. The restaurant was already booked and we had told the waiters that we were bringing a 'fish loving' customer. So they were all ready for that. Now we didn't have any time to change and re-adjust.

Mr Srinivasan was a pure vegetarian. He was getting uncomfortable by the smell of the restaurant itself. He was about to puke even. One of the waiters saw that and he said "Looks like this guy is drunk in the morning itself". Unfortunately, Srinivasan heard that and he shouted at the waiter. We took 5 minutes to pacify the auditor and lamented that these waiters sometimes behaved irresponsibly. They don't understand the work pressures being faced by a quality auditor, project manager and even a DP prime. I even cracked a joke about a waiter which I had received yesterday on WhatsApp. After 5 minutes, somehow Srini calmed down.

Now that one of their waiters goofed up, the restaurant manager was determined to impress the special guest. He asked his senior waiter to bring a glass box with a live fish to show him how fresh it was. Seeing this Srinivasan jumped out of his chair and ran out of the restaurant. We ran behind and somehow pacified him.

The construction workers having meals at the nearby roadside shop came running to check what the commotion was about. We somehow calmed down Srini. I even cracked the second joke I had from yesterday's WhatsApp message. Realizing Srini was a hard core veggie, we decided to buy some juice and banana from the roadside shop. The construction workers looked at us with amusement. We were wearing coat and suit and were eating rotten bananas. They thought we were kicked out from 'The Harbor' for not having money.

While walking back, I called my friend Sreejith and asked him to send some more jokes, which could be used in different situations during an audit, to my mobile. I congratulated myself for the thoughtful act.

The audit started.

Instead of our agenda, Srinivasan decided to follow his own agenda.

Sujay and I were already like the Indian side that had conceded 5 goals by halftime and were just waiting for the match to get over. Like in football, there is nothing like walkout and hence we had to wait for the audit to get over.

Srinivasan decided to do the lab audit first.

He entered the lab. Since we had told the team that the lab audit was only at the end and may be optional, team members as usual were having fun in wiring. One of the team members had just wired one setup and there was a wire which was lying on the ground. Srinivasan's legs got tangled in the wire and next thing we saw was Srinivasan flying and falling to the ground. The sound made the security guards come to the lab and we sent them away. His nose had hit the floor and it was bleeding. With the bleeding nose itself he had written something on the file—sure it was a NCR (Non Compliance).

Srinivasan asked: "Where is the first aid box in the lab?"

We searched for 5 minutes and finally unearthed an antique FA Box from a corner. It was being used as the base stand for a rat trap which facilities had kept after cleaning. I was sure that we had not opened that anytime in the recent past and we didn't clean it for the audit also. I opened the same and a cockroach family waiting for escape came out of it. Srinivasan jumped away. He again noted something in the file. I ran to the building reception and brought some plaster and cotton. With that somehow we dressed the nose of the auditor. After that, whatever he spoke became less clear.

Next thing he noticed was the Electro Static Discharge (ESD) machine in the lab. There is only one ESD in the whole company and that too doesn't work. We use it as a display item for audit and it will be moved from one lab to another during the visit through the back-door and before the auditor arrives. No one in the company knows how to operate it even. Since it's a mandatory requirement for the audit to pass, this process is followed year after year. Normally no auditors pay attention to the machine as well and everything ends on a happy note.

But, Srinivasan was furious after the 'Harbor' fiasco and he seemed determined to bring out all the potholes. He asked to switch on the ESD machine. With great reluctance but not showing it on the face, I switched it on. I was seriously thinking that the machine might not even get switched on. To my surprise, it got switched on and some numbers started showing in the display. Srinivasan handed over his files to Sujay and stood on the machine. He seemed to know how to operate the same. He turned some knob. Suddenly I saw Srinivasan shivering. First I thought he was becoming extremely happy to find a working machine, but soon realized that the second hand machine was giving an electric shock to our Auditor. I jumped and switched off the machine. Srinivasan had become red by now and he again noted something in his file. After the shock, hair on his head was standing straight up as if having goose bumps.

But that incident prompted Srinivasan to stop auditing the lab and he walked out finally. He decided to do the rest of the project audit.

By this time already quality department people were giving angry stares to me and Sujay.

The project audit started.

As decided, we opened our estimation model. But, Srinivasan was least interested in the same.

He asked us to open the project data. By this time Sujay and I had already made multiple prayers to different gods to have some sensible data. Hope Aravind's script had done some magic. To be precise, some sensible magic.

The data XL sheet was opened. I was happy to see that at least all the fields were populated.

Srinivasan asked, "How much time will it take you to complete a simple work item?"

"2 days approximately," Sujay answered.

But in the XL sheet, there was no simple item which was completed in 2 days. They were all showing more than a month. But at the same time all the complex items were getting completed in 2 days time. It seemed as if Aravind's script had collected the data but had mix matched the effort.

I realized the danger of this continuing further. It looked like project was already in CMM level minus 1 as per his observations. If he continued, it might go to CMM level minus 5. In that case, maybe we would be ok in 'absolute value' terms, but the useless quality department may still create problems. They are numerically challenged people.

So, I came out of the room as if going to the restroom. Then I went to the lab and plugged my mobile charger in the faulty electric point. The charger burnt but the purpose was achieved; the fire alarm burst. People were forced out of the building. Looks like even rats and cockroaches in Infopro are 'fire alarm' trained. I saw a bunch of rats and cockroaches rushing out of the lab. Even 2 snakes scrawled out behind them. Must be a snake family. The snakes worsened the situation. People ran helter-skelter after they saw the snakes. I saw the auditor Srini running laboriously in the middle of the crowd. I went just behind him and used my elbow to give one on the lower back of the running demon. He cried at once, in pain. Before he looked back, I had run in the other direction. He thought it was caused accidentally by someone in the running crowd.

I saw one of the snakes entering the wireless lab and the other one entering the Retail POS testing lab. I felt sad for the family — they got separated due to this absurd audit. So audits are harmful not only to the Project Manager and DP prime, but even for poor animals of this world.

I saw Srinivasan being taken away in a stretcher. He still had the NCR file tightly held in his hands.

Our eventful Audit finished with an "Un expected marathon".

Didn't know what the auditor wrote in the report. Anyways, our project became famous in Infopro. The project got adopted by the quality department. Srinivasan was in 'Ayush' Ayurveda care for 2 weeks.

Sujay and I were moved out of delivery. Both of us were transferred out of Bangalore and to northeast India. And, guess which department — Quality department.

Next week, we have to manage the external audit for one of the retail projects in Guwahati. When I heard the external auditor's name, a shiver ran down my spine — one Mr Srinivasan was flying down from Chennai for this audit!

2: The (Project) Delivery Pain

"*Chalo*, let's go for Project Meeting..." Aditi was screaming when I reached office.

It was quite unusual to have a project meeting on Wednesday morning because of two reasons. First of all, my Project Manager Sunny doesn't come to office at 9:00 AM. If at all he decides to come early, he will be in office by 11:00 AM; otherwise, he will be in just before lunch time. Secondly, Wednesday is rather considered as "execution day" in IT in which all the actions from Monday and Tuesday meetings get executed.

After throwing my backpack at my desk and switching on my PC, I also joined the trail of people rushing to the conference room. My laptop is one of the fastest in Infopro, it takes only 25 minutes to boot, so by the time I am back from the meeting, it should be up and running. Sunny was standing near the table, greeting everyone who enters the room. It seemed like he had not taken a bath as he had to reach office too early. I did not waste my time trying to guess from where the stinking smell was emanating.

Soon the project meeting started.

Sunny told, "Folks — I have a pleasant surprise for all of you — customer has just confirmed that they will give a new project to us. It is critical and needs to be completed soon."

The current project we were working involved maintaining the software of the distribution logic of a leading logistic company.

Sunny continued, "The new project is a development project in which some more logic needs to be added so that the company can ship more items. It also includes development of a web interface so that end users can choose the retail items to be shipped and the destination."

"So folks, this is a challenging project ('Challenge? for the developers for sure' I thought 'What challenge does a PM have after all?'). The project has some onsite chances for a few months, so some of you can look forward to that."

Hearing those words, two-three *laddoos* burst in me … I dreamt of sitting in Singapore Airlines and flying to California…

I could make out that many others in the room were also having similar dreams as very happy growling sounds were coming from different directions…

Sunny's words woke me up. "Shyju, You and few others have to work with me on the proposal for the same. We have to submit it by this Friday."

Next 2 days were full of white boarding, brainstorming and boot camps. Because of multiple writings and erasing, the white boards became almost black. Thus I should say, we even did black boarding sessions. Our project was good at maintenance (Well, customer may have a different opinion about how good are we in maintenance) but we never designed a new functionality.

As a customer oriented IT organization we should never say "I don't know". That is the unwritten rule in IT industry. No one will tell you that in as many words. You learn that the hard way.

So, though we did not have any experience in such a work item, we combined 10% knowledge, 50% assumptions, 30% guesses and 10% coin-tosses to arrive at the effort estimation. Many IT firms claim that they have an accurate estimation methodology, but most of them use the above method. Infopro is considering patenting the above method before others do.

As part of estimation, a lot of arrows and numbers were drawn in the board. Finally, the magic number revealed itself on the board. All the participants clapped and approved the figure!

We gave the estimation and schedule to the customer in 4 forms. An 80 page word document, a 30 slide PPT summary, a 4 'tab' XL and 2 page MS project. In the word doc, we included the company history, Google map from airport to company gate and some childhood photos of the Chairman. We copied some 40+ case studies from past RFP docs. We always give a lot of choice to the customer so that he can pick whichever he likes. Sunny was very particular that our proposal should be inferior to none!!! Sales folks even wanted to add a video of the estimation discussion in the ppt. But since most of us were not wearing formal dress and ties on most days, it was decided we will record it later and present it during the solution presentation.

While I could do only some random prayers and spiritual exercises, many people in the project had more innovative and practical ideas. Aditi started wearing more "attractive dress" like Menaka trying to get the attention of Viswamitra. She used to come with me for lunch, but she stopped it. And I saw her going with Sunny for lunch and even tea. I thought maybe I should also try to go with Sunny for lunch, which I tried the next day. For some reason, he became furious and asked me to complete the 'status report' before lunch and chased me away. When I looked back, he had started walking towards the cafeteria, cracking jokes with Aditi. Praveen's attendance record shot up from 6 hours a day to 12 hours a day which he achieved by spending 2 hours in cafeteria, 2 hours in the gym and 2 hours in front of the ladies college gate which is just outside our campus. But, the best among the lot was Suresh. He decided to pick-up and drop Sunny in his Maruti Zen car every day. Though Sunny had a car, chauffeur driven car is always a preferred option considering the driving conditions of Bangalore. Hence Sunny readily accepted it. I remembered that Suresh used to come only in bus complaining about Bangalore traffic. But he suddenly had picked up interest in driving to office!

After a few days, the news came — Infopro had won the project!!! It seems customer didn't have much time to evaluate and hence he decided to take some risks by assigning it to us. The other running dog DCS (Dynamic Consulting Services) had been kept away from the bone for now. Sunny sent a mail to the team congratulating the team and him-self. He copied the DM, VP and BU head and ensured that he received congrats mail from each of them. He moved all those mails to his 'Appreciations' folder.

While the celebrations went on for some days, what we didn't know was that the sales team had cut 30% of our estimate and given a 4 months effort instead of 6 months.

Customer informed that they wanted to consider the 4 months delivery scope as phase 1 and upon successful completion of the same, we would be considered for phase 2 which is a 2 year long project. It finally turned out that there is only one onsite chance for phase 1. Because of the 'close association' and 'excellent stakeholder management skills', Suresh was chosen to go onsite. The day when the roles of the new project were declared, the conference room resembled a Hindi serial. Different emotions were flowing freely through the faces of the people. Aditi complained of sudden headache, took a leave right after the meeting and left. She then extended the leave for the next 5 days. Praveen started packing his gym bags from 3:00 PM itself. I was chosen as the test lead from offshore. Since the new product is available only onsite, most of the development was supposed to happen from onsite. Suresh objected saying that most of the development work is simple and offshore people can login remotely and work. He would do the co-ordination, which is more difficult! But, Sunny told him the customer wanted it that way. Suresh was not very happy with that but had to finally settle for it.

During the next few days, Suresh walked around putting salt in most of our wounds. He called Aditi and asked about the list of shopping malls in Fremont, California which she was proactively collecting. He secretly asked me about the "night life" in California which one day he had found me reading about.

Suresh decided to throw an onsite party at Amul joint inside the campus. That day Aditi didn't come to office. Praveen later told he is not well. I initially thought of not going but decided to go and take the revenge on him. I myself ordered 10 chocolates, 5 ice-creams and 3 sandwiches all at the highest price. I packed the unfinished ones to take home with me.

Finally Suresh reached the customer site and the project officially started.

In the first week itself Sunny got a customer complaint that Suresh had stared at the receptionist and every day he called the customer director's secretary 5 times for some or the other reason.

Sunny asked Suresh about it and he told he was calling the secretary to get his access badge done. When Sunny told Suresh that he had already been given his badge on the first day his answer was that some of the doors were not opening. Since there was no further evidence available from onsite for this, the case ended without any action, much to the disappointment of Aditi, me and Pravin. Pravin even secretly tried to collect some evidence against the culprit. Anyway, after that, Suresh knew that the secretary was not ready to open any more doors for him.

Since our sales had given a 2 months' 'on the spot discount' in delivery time, our schedule had to be shrunk. Since there was no time to rework the plan, Sunny reduced the time of all the activities uniformly. The original 'waterfall model' we planned now transformed itself into an 'agile model', in which all the phases were overlapping. So, before we complete design, we will start coding and before coding completion, we will start testing.

First week of the status report looked great! Everything was green with the status as 'initiated'. Sunny even put a smilie at the end of the status PPT J. He even sent a copy of the 'green' status report to the DM and VP and duly moved the reply mails to his 'Appreciations' folder.

Next two weeks were design weeks. Suresh was supposed to work on this. He told he was sick for 3 days because of the California climate. But, later he posted his photos in Facebook standing in front of Disneyland and Universal Studios in LA.

After 1.5 weeks of hard work, Suresh sent the Design_Document_v0.1. The document looked more like a template with <TBD> in most of the places and more than 90% of the document empty.

Since the document needed to be delivered in the next 2 days, Sunny suggested using the ultimate weapon 'Google' to find some content.

Miraculously Suresh delivered a 100 page document the next day. Sunny sent an appreciation note to Suresh for going 'beyond miles' and delivering as expected. The document was finally sent to the customer for review.

Customer review came back with more comments than the content itself. The final comment from the customer in bold red letters was that someone had copied this entire document to Wikipedia! For some or the other reason, Suresh's document looked the same as the Wikipedia content for the same technology. The first 20 pages were the 'History of logistics'. The next 30 pages were about logistics industry with pictures. The next 50 pages talked about different technology used in the industry.

Suresh complained that the customer was creating a hostile environment intentionally. He even told that DCS had placed a good looking sales girl onsite and hence the customer was trying to create problems for us. He told that henceforth, he himself would take care of the reviews and need not have to go to customer at all.

Soon, coding started. Suresh became frequently sick. But his WhatsApp and Facebook updates also increased. The photos from Napa Valley, Grand Canyon, Lake Tahoe, Yosemite, etc., also started appearing.

I started telling Sunny that coding was getting delayed. But Sunny said that Suresh was working hard and whenever he called he could hear the typing sound of the keyboard and he also showed the mails sent by Suresh at 2:00 AM in the night. I was completely shattered by the evidence and came back disappointed.

In the next project meeting, Sunny told the offshore team to offer some extended help to Suresh as he was working very hard. As the Senior tester, I asked for the current status of the coding. In his reply, Suresh only asked for the test plan from my side. I told him we could not make a test plan with the sub-standard design document which was there. After exchange of a few un-parliamentary (or may be un-IT) words between us, I walked out of the project meeting.

Next day, I got a meeting invite from Sunny which looked like below.

Organizer: Sunny Joseph

Subject: Mid-term feedback

Venue: Dinosaur conference room

Time: 10:00 AM–11:00 AM

In the midterm feedback, I was told that I was not customer oriented and neither was I a good team player. Besides, it seems one of the team members had complained that I wasted the meeting's effectiveness by asking frivolous questions.

Sunny soon published a recovery plan for the project. The summary of that said that Suresh would be doing all heavy work items like saving the code in the right folder, writing proper comments in the code, etc., while relatively simple tasks of writing and testing the code would be done by two software engineers who had newly joined. It seems it was Suresh's suggestion to have this plan as SEs would get better enabled for the phase 2 of the program.

Sunny also prepared a status report saying that though the whole project was in red, the plan for recovery was in place and he promptly put the status of the plan as 'green' with status as 'initiated'. It is customary in IT that every project plan will be 'glaring green' in its first week. The status will read 'initiated' against every item. If you are good in fooling your superiors, you can run the plan with 'In progress' status (glaring green colour) for a few more weeks.

Planning, Re-planning, Planning to Plan, etc. ... happened on a daily basis. Finally, the code completion date arrived. The two SEs had not seen the sun-light for past 3-4 days as they were living in the office. One of them fainted the day before and Sunny took him to the clinic inside the campus. The doctor asked him to take rest. But Sunny promptly reminded the doctor that if he travelled to his home in the traffic, he would be more tired and hence it was best for him to stay in the office and complete the code.

It seems the final integration compile of the code broke 10 times. Finally, Suresh took the intelligent decision to comment the whole file-out rather than fixing the error. Next day was testing start day. When I came in the morning itself already there are 25 mails in my mail-box congratulating Suresh and team for completing the coding milestone. I went to the bottom of the mail chain. Sunny's original mail had entire 1 paragraph about the contributions of Suresh. Unfortunately Sunny made cut paste mistake and the bottom of the mail was still saying 'Rgds, Suresh' meaning Suresh himself had written the mail.

As test-lead, I started testing the code. After loading the code the entire production test setup came to a halt. The system hung and the entire database crashed. It was so powerful that some of the servers sitting near our server also crashed!!! It seems the Data Centre operator even saw smoke coming out of our server. I raised a priority 1 issue. But upon Sunny talking to Suresh, he told this was a minor issue and asked me to close the issue immediately. He told these were simple issues which the SEs could easily look into.

The next 4 days, the SEs were deprived of sun-light and even food. Suresh was not reachable the whole week as he went for vacation after a 'tight schedule'. His Facebook started showing the updates and photographs from Florida.

After one of the SEs came and told that he would either become a mental patient or would commit suicide, Sunny finally called a system architect from another project. He managed to fix the problem in a day. The root cause he gave was that it seems one important file was commented fully.

I again started testing. For every test case, there were 2 bugs which were found. By evening, already 100 bugs were raised. Seeing the situation, the two SEs sneaked out through the back door of the building when Sunny went to the bathroom. One of them threw a folded paper into the campus from outside the company boundary wall. The security picked it up and brought it to me. It was his resignation letter. Their mobiles were found switched off from then onwards till the whole week.

Next Monday morning Suresh returned from vacation. He told Sunny that the testing team was testing all un-wanted scenarios. Sunny asked me to close more than half of the issues, I refused. I was again given a feedback session and told that I was not working for the cause of the team.

Since the end date was nearing, it was decided to put the code in beta testing directly. Few of the customer sites in the US were chosen for this. The next week was an unforgettable week for many of the US cities.

It seems several of marriages in the US got cancelled as instead of bridal wear, they got underwear delivered. If people ordered laptop, they got spinning tops. For a church where a funeral mass was going on, instead of flowers, chocolates and cake got delivered. A grandmother who ordered a church scarf got a sexy bikini delivered. Somebody ordered a music CD, they got an adult CD (It seems, after that the number of CD ordering increased in the US). Someone ordered for dog biscuit and got rat poison delivered. It seems the US president got 3 pairs of sandals delivered (Suresh later told that it was a correct delivery).

Within 2 days, the beta deployment was stopped and rolled-back. It seems even the US Vice President called the client CEO from Washington DC to request a roll back.

The sales and project delivery team did separate Root Cause Analysis (RCA) for the same. Delivery's RCA said Sales reduced the project duration without consulting them. Sales RCA said delivery screwed this up despite the sales winning the project against extreme competition from DCS.

Ultimately, between design team and test team, they decided that the root cause was that the test team didn't test the code properly.

The customer had no confusion in making the decision for Phase 2. The phase 2 went to DCS.

Sunny and I got lower performance rating.

Suresh got appreciation from the customer for handling a tight project at onsite. He got a special bonus from our BU head. A week after the bonus, he resigned from Infopro and joined DCS as the onsite coordinator. He got 30% additional salary hike as well.

Last update in his Facebook says he has submitted all papers for green card processing.

3: Customer Devo Bhava

The Taittiriya Upanishad says that one must consider his *Maata* (Mother), *Pitaa* (Father), Guru (Teacher) and *Atithi* (Guest) as gods. For unknown reasons, the Upanishad did not include 'customers' in that list.

It was actually Infopro Limited, who identified this basic mistake and included 'customers' in the prestigious group. Our chairman had suggested to the HRD ministry to issue the next version of the Upanishad incorporating the above correction.

While we are still waiting for the change to be made, my customer decided to visit Infopro. Since I am the PM for the customers' project, he is going to be my guest on July 10th and 11th Monday and Tuesday. As he is a customer as well as a guest, as per my company policy, he was more than a god!

I booked hotel rooms, sight-seeing trips and dinner at best restaurants for him and his team. I had made sure that the dinner booking included few of us also as this was one golden chance to party at the expense of Infopro. After Infopro had stopped the yearly team building fund, teams had used customer visits as the opportunity to do some relaxing using company money. Last but not the least I had to take care of the gifts for the customers. I really wanted to order a memory stick. This is another opportunity for the organizers to receive some free gifts. Usually we order one or two extra and the non-gifted ones logically belong to the organizer. However, the unit finance manager (UFM—should have been called UFO as he always behaves alien to the company) told no more budget for this customer visit as it had already crossed the limit. Arguing with him was no use and hence with the available budget I ordered a coffee mug and a T-shirt with Infopro logo on them.

The client firm is the Cyprus based 'Tom & Jerry Aviation Experts' (TJAE) who make sensors for the aircraft makers.

TJAE is a small firm. For 'case study' purposes, we consider the company as a 'fortune 25000' company. They make the sensors for measuring the atmospheric conditions, wind speed, etc., and report it on the cockpit dashboard. The sensors they produce belong to the low profile category — the ones which the pilots usually don't use for taking any major decisions.

Tom and Jerry founded the company 15 years back when they were thick friends. Of late, the relationship soured. Jerry is the CEO and Tom, the COO. Jerry brought in his younger brother Bill as his Executive Assistant after Bill had failed his graduation exam the 5th time. Tom objected as he thought maybe Jerry planned to make Bill the next CEO. Jerry told the press that Bill was brought in because he was a 'professional' and not because he was the brother of the founder. Tom brought in Eric, his nephew as his EA. Eric had taken voluntary retirement from education after 8th grade.

The Executive Assistants also brought some of their own initiatives to the company. Bill thought the recruitment process of the company was not correct. Hence he published the question paper of the company's recruitment on the internet so that candidates could prepare and come. While Eric heard from somewhere that everything could be automated. So, he first tried to automate the company's sales force system. He had found that sales people were doing nothing but calling and sending mails to the customers. As per the new automation, this would be done in regular sequence by a script. Unfortunately the script writer made a mistake in the script in the day's calculation. First day of the script run, each customer got 1000 mails and 200 calls and half of them sent a termination notice to TJAE.

The above developments combined with many other such incidents created bitter differences of opinion between Tom and Jerry and they were seen fiercely arguing with each other in their cabins. In recent times, the moment they see each other, verbal duels ensue. They had stopped short of slapping each other with brooms and throwing plates at each other just as the original Tom and Jerry would have done when they were angry.

Jerry outsourced some IT work to Infopro whereas Tom preferred BTS (Bharatiya Technology Solutions), our cross town competitor to outsource all IT testing work. Last month, there was yet another Tom & Jerry show in their headquarters. The quarrel started between the two Executive Assistants, Bill and Eric, and the bosses took over from the EAs. They were on the verge of a split. As part of the compromise formula, many portfolios changed hands. It was decided that Tom take over all outsourcing works to India and hence Tom became our boss since then.

Let's come to the main point of discussion, i.e., Tom, the COO of TJAE is visiting us. In the past, he always favoured our rival BTS and he is visiting Infopro for the first time, to evaluate us.

After he took over the relationship with Infopro, Tom had started reviewing our program closely and had raised a number of concerns. He wanted to junk Jerry's decision to give the work to us. My BDM told me that he is coming to India to wrap up the project in Infopro and announce his decision to transition it to BTS.

I was an acting PM for the project and not promoted as a PM officially. My boss—Group Manager Raghu Srinivasan—told me that I didn't have the assertiveness and the quality to lead from the front! He had asked me to be the acting PM for this new project and prove myself. The last project I had managed had goofed up. I sincerely believe that the goof up did not happen because of me, but because of my colleagues, my manager, HR and the client—at least that is what I believe. Getting a good rating this year was absolutely necessary for me to keep my job and to get a promotion and salary hike.

I had booked a flat in Pannareddy & Co's latest project on Hosur Road. Since none of the flats were falling within my budget and loan availability, I had to settle for a drainage facing 900 square feet 2 BHK on ground floor, which nobody else wanted to book. I'd given the advance. The further payments on that were dependent on me continuing in the job.

So, all in all, the visit of Tom was going to be a turning point in my life, mostly for worse.

Since the COO was coming down, my BU head, Radhakrishna (RK, as others call him), also decided to join the customer meeting.

On the day of the visit, all of us were dressed in our best. I'd borrowed a suit from the dhobi in my neighbourhood. At 9:00 AM, HR manager Shiva, GM Raghu, I and RK lined up outside the main gate to receive Tom.

Tom, along with Eric, disembarked from his car and we exchanged greetings and started walking towards the HQ block for the scheduled meetings. For some reason, no one was talking. Tom decided to break the silence.

Tom noticed the street dog which was standing under the shade near the gate. He just wanted to initiate the conversation. "Nice dog ... what is his breed?" he asked RK, the BU head.

RK, who was busy framing a question about the weather, stopped midway (It is a customary practice in our company to ask any visiting client about the weather, irrespective of whether he has come from the Arctic or the Sahara). RK had seen that dog near the gate several times, but had never thought about which breed it belonged to. Apart from claiming that his company delivers best of 'breed' java code, he had never thought about any other breeds. So, he looked at GM Raghu, his way of passing the question. Raghu gave a surprised look at the dog and uttered "Yeah... super nice dog." He then looked at the HR Manager, Shiva, i.e., he too passed the question.

Shiva thought for a moment about which department in Infopro deals with dogs. His friend in HR Shilpa had told him once that "I have to deal with these dogs day in day out". He thought of contacting Shilpa and asking, but he suddenly figured out another way.

HR Manager looked at me, the PM (Poor Manager), and passed on the question to me.

I looked at the security, who was standing by the side.

Security looked at the dog.

And the dog looked at the client. Information cycle was complete!

Dog was wondering "These guys look very gentlemanly and knowledgeable. But they don't even know my breed..." He wanted to say loudly "I belong to the social class of 'the great Indian Street Dog'... *Yaani ki... 'Bharatiya Aaavara Kutta'*..." He couldn't speak, so he just barked.

Since everybody was now looking at the dog, and the dog was barking, security sensed that the dog maybe about to attack. He wanted to score a brownie point. He too was waiting for a confirmation in his job. He picked up a stone and threw it at the dog. Though the security person had gone through rigorous training at the Security Training Institute of Infopro, throwing stone at a dog was not included in the syllabus. As a result, the stone missed its target and instead hit Tom's groin.

He was groaning in pain, but somehow controlled himself.

My BU head was a champion of 'customer delight' and he wanted to massage wherever the stone was hit, but quickly he backtracked. He did not want to be misunderstood by his subordinates.

The *Economics Today* channel reporter, who was loitering around the Infopro HQ, immediately took pictures of the dog, the body part of the client where the stone hit and the security person and started dictating some breaking news to his channel.

It took half a minute for Tom to recoup and come back to normal. He decided to ignore his previous question. Knowing the breed of the street dog was least of his priorities anyway, but saving his 'vital parts' from getting damaged was definitely a priority. So he decided to walk towards the building as soon as possible.

There was silence everywhere. RK was happy that now he could ask about the weather and keep the conversation going.

"So Mr Tom, how is the weather in Cyprus?" (GM Raghu got disappointed at this as he was actually planning to ask that question when his turn comes. He decided to modify his question and ask about the weather of Dubai, Tom's transit point).

"In the morning, a lot of dew." Tom started describing Cyprus weather. "When the sun peaks, few spells of high humidity and dry winds. Pleasant evening. Lot of sensor complaints from customers."

Now that was a googly of an answer. Actually RK did not want so many details. He had expected Tom to say that the weather was cold or hot or that it was raining. He had actually prepared the follow-up questions and statements for the above 3 responses only. But he was clean-bowled by Tom's response. He got confused whether to say 'Oh nice weather' or 'So sorry … you should be spending more time in Bangalore before leaving for Cyprus' — the only 2 options he had thought about in his mind as the initial response.

As he got stuck, he had to move to plan B, which was a question about the food in the hotel Tom was staying.

"How was your dinner at hotel yesterday? I am sure you enjoyed the Indian cuisine."

"Dinner… Paneer tickka… Stomach upset… No sleep… toilet full night." It was answered by Eric, the EA, who could not speak English well.

Tom was a bit embarrassed.

RK was still thinking how to respond to this. Should I say "No worries … we have a clinic within campus, you can pick up some lemotils…" or should I say "you can have lunch from our cafeteria and the motion will stop completely for the next 4-5 days until you safely reach Cyprus."

But RK is very sharp. He had found out other options too.

He immediately changed the course of the walk, took Tom to the nearby corridor and showed the board 'Toilet'.

"See … we have our toilets here on this side … just remembered showing you this right away."

Tom looked at RK's face. Tom's face showed a mix of anger and embarrassment. He looked at the Executive Assistant and said something in Cyprus language. Believe me, you don't need to be a PM in Infopro to understand that it was the highest available abusive word in Cyprus language.

RK was happy that he quickly and clearly understood the customer requirements and responded with utmost speed. He felt proud of himself. "I should narrate this customer delight story in my next interview with *Economics Today*." He asked the GM to make a note. Raghu always walks around with a notebook. He was happy to help the BU Head with the note.

After 2 eventful minutes, we reached the conference room.

As soon as we got seated in the room, HR manager Shiva gave him the gift—a beautiful coffee mug and a T-shirt.

"The coffee mug is made from Rajasthan porcelain and silicon from Ceylon. It will never break," Shiva told proudly as he poured the hot coffee into Tom's brand new mug.

One of the legs of the conference room table was shorter. As we in Infopro are trained in positive thinking, we used to say that the 3 legs are lengthier and the 4th one normal. Though we are positive thinkers, the damn table is not. Because of the slight discrepancy in 3-dimensional symmetry, the table tilted 3 degrees, when Tom's tummy touched the table edge. The coffee mug fell on the table first and then on Tom's shirt and then on the ground.

The unbreakable mug broke into pieces and all the coffee spilled over Tom's white shirt.

HR manager Shiva came running and apologized. He pleaded with Tom to remove his shirt and put on the new Infopro T-shirt which we gifted. Tom agreed.

Someone had told me Tom is a short guy and I had chosen the T-shirt size accordingly. However he was 6' 1'' and appeared short only because he was very fat.

Tom put on the T-Shirt. It was too short for him. It could cover only till 3 inches above his navel. He looked like Rakhi Sawant getting ready for an item dance.

Eric, Tom's EA, liked the outfit. "Nice Bikini … Bollywood fashion … very good … yesterday TV song." He approved his boss's latest fashion statement. He thought that the cloth was actually designed that way.

Tom was not sure if he should remove the T-shirt or not. The T-shirt was so tight and to remove it, the only way out was to cut it using scissors. Since his shirt was already taken by the security to wash, he had only 2 options. Either take off the T-shirt by cutting or tearing and sit there like Salman Khan — showing all his 6 packs. Or next option was to keep at least the 2 critical packs covered with Infopro T-shirt and sit there in the Rakhi Sawant-style attire, exposing remaining 4 packs!

Like an average Indian man, he chose Rakhi Sawant over Salman Khan.

As the customer sat there uncomfortably clad in bikini top, the conversations started. Once in a while he unsuccessfully tried to extend the T-shirt to cover his stomach. He required somewhat 5 metre cloth to cover his belly comfortably — but what we gave him was a 45 centimetre cloth piece. That was quite symbolic of how we used to deliver our software against customer's requirements.

Tom introduced himself and his EA and exchanged cards.

Then he started talking about a wonderful vehicle he had seen on the roads of Bangalore — he said it was missing its 4th wheel, nevertheless, it was able to go as fast as a Jumbo Jet. It was 'compact, flexible and agile'. He had never seen such an efficient vehicle in Cyprus.

"I even saw that this compact vehicle could jump from the service road to main highway over a 4 feet wide open drainage. That is a great flight capacity. I would like to know more about the aviation technology used in that vehicle." Not only that vehicle could pierce any traffic jam with enormous precision even though sometime it makes minor scratches to some of the cars nearby.

And he fired the final salvo "You should run your project like that vehicle — agile, flexible and compact, which can fly from one critical path to another one without complaining of hurdles."

RK asked Raghu to note the point. HR too noted the same and immediately instructed his recruitment team to recruit some consultants who were experienced with the compact, flexible, agile vehicle on the Bangalore roads.

I started thinking about what all changes to bring about in my project so that it could be run like an auto-rickshaw. My GM Raghu was already like a rude rickshaw driver. Raghu asks more from each of us. He wants us to work late nights and weekends. At least some features are matching, I thought.

"We will surely get some experts and consultants to talk to you about that technology," RK assured Tom. "We will send the slide deck and case studies to you by Sunday evening." Then he looked at me "Venky ... you take the action to do more research on the technology of the vehicle and send the slide ware by Sunday evening. I will review it by Saturday evening." I nodded my head.

"Why don't we start the presentations? I have a meeting with Nasdaq officials at 11:00 AM." RK wanted to show that he was too busy and that he was also a high profile man.

"Shall we start with slides on business transformation using cloud"? Raghu asked enthusiastically. His eyes were on Tom's protruding stomach and navel.

"No." Tom did not like the idea. He tried to extend the T-shirt to cover his stomach as he felt uncomfortable with Raghu's staring.

"If you don't like cloud, we have a very interesting slide deck on analytics. Shall we?"

That also was shot down.

"OK. We have a very good presentation on our company history, values, our chairman's quotes, etc. We can finish that quickly."

"No. Let's review the project." Tom appeared to be in a hurry.

"But, as per the agenda I circulated yesterday, our project review is between 2:30 PM to 2:55 PM" I intervened. I had kept the project review immediately after the lunch so that people would be sleepy.

"No, let's get straight into the project review. I know the history of your company as I get to hear that quite often." The decibel level of Tom soared north. "I don't get anything from your history, but let me see if you can do something for me in the 'present'."

Tom continued. His face turned red now. "We had actually given the requirement to build 100 sensors which can capture the acoustic waves in the ultrasonic range so that it can identify the presence of some birds even at a 3 kilometre distance. That would be fixed at the tail and would have been a great safety device." Tom continued. "In requirement 2, we wanted 100 smoke detectors — to be fixed in aircraft toilets."

"Your team has sent us 200 sensors last week."

"Oh that is great." My BU Head had still not guessed where the story was going. He looked at Raghu and me appreciatively. I held my breath.

"Out of the 200 sensors, 150 did not pass the initial screening test. It's completely useless."

GM Raghu looked at me angrily.

"Oh, that happens once in a while. The airport staff does not handle these delicate sensors well," RK told casually. "I will raise this point in my next meeting with the aviation ministry."

"We wanted the bathroom sensors to detect smoke and the tail-end sensors to detect the specific acoustic signals so that the presence of birds at long distance could be identified. You guys have used the specification of the smoke-detecting-sensor for the tail-end sensors and the special sound detection sensor in the toilets."

And you know what happened in our beta testing. The pilot switched on the sensors after takeoff. Immediately afterwards a fat Sardarji entered the toilet. All 'acoustic' signals were amplified and played back in the cockpit. The co-pilot fainted as he was allergic to the sounds of specific type. Suddenly the smoke detector at the tail also became active due to the engine smoke. All red alerts in the flight went off. There was total chaos in the plane. Red alert was sent to all airports in Cyprus and the CIA also picked up some of those signals and their aircraft carrier fleet in the Mediterranean rushed towards Cyprus.

RK looked at me with his eyes bulged out and mouth wide open. He was in total disbelief. He was not taking his eyes off me. Was he in awe of me because of the huge impact of what my project had delivered or was he trying to set me on fire by the sharp hot beams of light from the corner of his eyes? Even CIA had taken note of my project deliverables. Hopefully no one will tell me I don't have any 'visibility'.

When BU head continued to stare at me, I panicked and started trembling. I am losing my job for sure.

The 50,000 Rs booking amount I had already paid for the ground floor, drainage-facing 2 BHK was going down the drain.

Pannareddy & Co builders was not going to return me the money.

I felt like being captured by cannibals in a distant Amazonian forest village, who had thrown me into the frying pan. The cannibals were dancing around the pan with spears in their hands.

Tom, head of the cannibals, was shouting at the top of his lungs. I wanted to have company with me in the frying pan. I thought of my architect 'Dharani'. I have heard that sharing sadness will halve it and sharing happiness will double it. I thought I should share the customer wrath with Dharani so that, well, maybe it will save my job at least.

"Well, Tom, I understand the concern," I started with a stammer. "I understand that there were issues with the testing team from BTS who could not do the Integration testing properly. I won't blame the testers in BTS. Since BTS always recruits from Tier-4 institutes and pays them peanuts, they don't get the best breed of people like us in Infopro." I tried to deflect the blame to BTS. "As you rightly said, we need a detailed discussion. I have asked Dharani, my architect, to join the meeting. He is on his way."

I thought about ways to put all the blame on someone else. As I was too tense, no good ideas came up in my mind.

While we waited for Dharani to arrive, my GM got Prashant from advanced technology team to give an exciting presentation on cloud and analytics. This time, he did not care to ask Tom. As soon as Prashant came to the room, GM just announced "Let's utilize this time for some extremely useful information presentation on the latest buzzwords 'cloud' and 'analytics'."

Prashant had 275 slides on cloud and 234 on analytics and he apologized in the beginning that the slide ware is still work in progress.

Tom was completely uninterested. But he thought of being polite and acting as if he was interested. For the first few slides, he asked a few questions as well. Such as— "What is the font size you have used?", "Is it MS Office 2010 or 2007?," etc.

In between Raghu turned back and looked at me "You have goofed up this project also. I can't believe… Be ready to find another job." Then he sent an SMS to someone. I hoped it was not to my Unit HR.

When the cloud was in slide 38, I went out, called Dharani and gave him the details of Tom's concerns. I asked him to think and prepare well for the discussion.

By the time Dharani came in, Prashant was on slide 73. Except Prashant and me everyone in the room was sleeping. Customer was in semi coma state. I couldn't sleep because I was worried about the job.

As Dharani came in and rushed towards me sitting in one corner, his hand hit the table. The table tilted 3 degrees based on the 3-dimensional asymmetry and the laptop fell on Tom. He woke up from the semi coma state.

To show that he was carefully listening all along, Tom asked a question to Prashant.

"Can we have a virtual cloud embedded in the sensors?"

Prashant took some time to digest the question. RK showed him some sign language using his eyes and fingers. So Prashant spoke up.

"We will do it for you sir. We can embed anything Sir. We have a CoE for sensors, another CoE for embedded systems and we have a practice for cloud. We will collaborate between all the 3 and make a winning proposal for you. Can we send our consultants to Cyprus next week to study your requirement Sir?" Prashant paused for a moment to breathe.

"Oh. Nice, nice ... we will talk about it later." Tom was not interested to continue further on that topic. "As we have all the stakeholders lets continue our review of the ongoing project."

Prashant was disappointed. He anyway had to rush out of the room as he had another presentation at 11:30 AM at the weather department headquarters in Bangalore. The topic was "Predicting 'cloud' movements using 'analytics' and saving the data in a compact 'cloud' built by Infopro". The weather department guys were eagerly waiting for the presenter as it was news to them that the tech company could manufacture cloud and even store some data there.

So, now all eyes were back on us—me and Dharani. I was terribly tensed.

Cannibals started their spear-dancing and song. The third cannibal, Raghu Srinivasan, even had a long sword apart from the spear.

"What is that *dhak-dhak* sound—your mobile?" Raghu pointed to my shirt pocket.

Actually it was the sound of my heart thumping with fear and tension. I tried hard to control it, but the volume level only went up.

As we took centre stage, Tom repeated the accusations once again. I looked at Dharani as if he was responsible for the entire mess.

"Tom, you know the basic principles we adopted for the project was that of future proof design and innovation as a service (IAAS)..." Dharani cleared his throat and started.

Tom was hearing the above for the first time. But he did not want to show his 'ignorance'.

"Yes I agree," he said.

I was wondering when the above decision was made and what is meant by 'Innovation as a Service'.

"This project was originally given to Global IT Solutions Limited in Cyprus to make the sensors." Dharani continued confidently "They outsourced this portion to us and later TJAE took over the Global IT Solutions. As they are not well versed with English, they made a fundamental mistake when they wrote 'the specifications of the toilet smoke detecting sensor and acoustic signal detectors respectively are as follows...' And, then they interchanged the specifications."

I did not recall any such errors. But decided to agree with Dharani.

"Tom, you know what. Jerry was handling the project from TJAE at that time, he overlooked it. He does not have the attention to detail like you have." Tom was elated. That dumb head Jerry should have been here in this meeting — he thought.

Dharani continued — "We had actually done some research on the topic. We found that in 1960, one of the Pan Guinean flights had a sound detector near the toilet. It helped one of their pilots to overhear a secret conversation between two hijackers and he could avoid the hijack of the plane by landing back at the airport immediately."

"Oh I see…" Tom was more interested. "Ok... I agree sound detection in toilet can be very useful! What about the smoke detector at the tail?" Tom was eager.

"If there are damages on the outer coat of the plane surface, there could be sparks due to friction. This happened with a Mauritian flight while flying over the Sahara. A smoke detector on every 1 square metre of plane surface can come handy in such situations."

"Also, what we have made is a universal sensor. It can be fixed in any part of the plane. We implemented only one functionality in each of the sensors. If you give us a green signal, we will implement the other circuitry also and you will have a 2-in-one sensor of which you can activate any one of the functionality. You may please send back all sensors; we will activate the second circuitry in them also. We will send you the additional cost details."

Dharani paused to assess Tom's reaction. He looked confused, but was slowly getting impressed with Dharani's explanation. "I know Jerry may not understand the technical details, but I am sure you can very well understand the intricacies and innovation involved." Tom's face glowed.

"I know your investors have started asking you to replace Jerry as the CEO. Your technical prowess will come handy when you take over." Tom's face glowed more. He had actually never heard about any investors asking him to be the CEO. But he did not think too much. He was happy about what he just heard.

Cannibals had now stopped the spear dance.

I thought it was time to speak up and collect a few brownie points for myself.

"See, BTS did the end to end testing for this. Though their project does not have a good PM, they still gave a good try," I started. "But they could not match the speed of deliverables going out of our team as I took extreme care to run the project as well-oiled machinery."

"You can perhaps ask them to get a good PM like in Infopro or maybe that part of the program can be given to us. Project Management in Infopro is one of the best in the industry." I looked at the GM. He had to nod his head in agreement.

Dharani took over from me with the perfection of a relay race. "Since BTS doesn't have the domain knowledge, they are not in a position to do the validations properly. They are just looking at it as a piece of electronic circuit, whereas it is not. The testers should look at it as a safety device. TJAE gives utmost importance to their customers and is 100% committed to air safety. BTS should understand that."

"Then only they will be able to come up with the right test scenarios and do a good job of validation," Dharani quickly finished his competitor-bashing pitch.

"Just look at this… As per BTS policy, they consider customers as Kings. We consider customers as God. That itself is a great differentiator." I tried to collect a few more bonus points.

My BU head was quiet all this time and suddenly, for some reason, he also became intelligent. "You know, we are about to start our new practice for sensor validation services and we would like you to inaugurate it today. We will start validation of all your sensors and softwares from our own world class facility."

"But the validation part is with BTS now," Tom mumbled.

"Well, we can present the transition plan by tomorrow — to transition all work from BTS to Infopro."

"But…" Tom was about to say something. I stared at his bare navel. Raghu also joined me. He became uncomfortable again and tried to pull his T-shirt to cover his navel. He could not complete what he was about to say.

As Tom was busy adjusting his wardrobe, RK did not waste a minute. "It will be our extreme pleasure to get you as the inaugurator for our Sensor Validation Practice. If it was Jerry in your place, I would not have invited him for this," RK continued.

"We usually invite BBMP corporators for such big events." Tom was pleased. He thought BBMP corporator is the ultimate group of 'celebrity leaders' who are invited for big events and inaugurations.

CEO turned to HR "Call the press reporter who was standing outside. We will have a joint press release."

Tom was about to say something but he held back as Raghu started staring at his navel again. He was a bit confused but by looking at the enthusiasm around the room, he also got elated. 'Rather than getting into minute details, I should take it as an opportunity to outscore over Jerry. In the next AGM, I can show it as an achievement on my part, i.e., consolidation of vendors. Dumb head Jerry should be pushed out of the CEO's chair.'

HR Manager called the facilities manager and asked him to clear a portion of the cafeteria and prepare an 'inauguration setup' and a board reading 'Sensor Validation Services Practice'. Tom was taken in a golf cart and he did the inauguration. A lot many people gathered to see the customer in an 'Infopro Bikini top'. They took pictures. Tom felt elated and happy.

In the evening, we took him to the best 5-star bar in town. We again spoke about the ill treatment meted out to them by BTS, how BTS recruits 4th class people in their projects and also about why Tom is a born CEO material, whereas Jerry is a dumb head.

I also spoke about why the crap project managers in BTS were letting their clients down and how the brilliant PMs in Infopro had been delivering customer delights day in and day out.

Tom, in his inebriated state, verbally agreed to my statements. I recorded it in my mobile phone so that I could attach the .avi file in my next appraisal form. After each statement, I looked at Raghu and he nodded in agreement. I wanted to capture that in my mobile video camera but that did not work out.

After the visit, Tom went back to Cyprus. He was supposed to visit BTS after Infopro, which he cancelled.

We published the photo of Tom inaugurating the 'Sensor Validation Practice' in Infopro and asked the scribe to write a story about a 'rumour in the industry circle' about how TJAE was going to give all their validation work to Infopro instead of BTS and also about how the testers from BTS had already started flowing to Infopro. It also talked about rumours of impending layoffs in testing group of BTS.

The next Sunday, we kept a walk-in interview for testers and almost 80% of the BTS testers joined us.

BTS testing delivery suffered further and TJAE was more angry with them now.

Next month, we got the Purchase Order from TJAE for all validation services. Got 8 million USD worth of additional business for that year.

Sensor manufacturing and Validation is the new high-flying practice in Infopro.

GM Raghu was scolded by BU head RK for not identifying such a golden opportunity earlier. He asked Raghu to have his ears tuned to the ground. When I returned from the coffee room, I saw Raghu lying on the floor with his left ear touching the ground as if he was trying to hear some noise from the floor. I did not understand why.

RK appreciated me and Dharani for the world class innovation and customer satisfaction. He asked the marketing team to prepare a brochure on 'Innovation as a Service'. Both of us got double promotion. I became Senior Group Manager and Dharani became Principal Architect. GM was demoted in his role. He was asked to manage the English training program for the Burundi-based toilet cleaning company.

I went to Pannareddy Constructions and replaced my drainage-facing-2 BHK with the garden facing 3 BHK on the 9th floor. I decided to resell my 2 BHK to GM Raghu. I told him it was a very lucky flat. As soon as I booked it, I got customer appreciation and double promotion and we got more work for Infopro. Though he covered his nose when he came near the drainage, he appeared convinced that it was a very lucky flat.

A few months later, Raghu invited everyone to the house warming ceremony of his drainage facing flat. I skipped the event as I am allergic to drainage smell of late. I heard many people vomited at his house warming because of the stinky smell.

It is already 2 years since Raghu started staying in his flat. However, luck has not dawned on him even till yesterday 8:00 PM when I called him to ask to send me the 10 page status report in the next 1 hour.

4: Gavaskar Hates Cricket

Gavaskar was kicked on his ass by Kapil Dev. Gavaskar retired hurt. He resolved he will never again play cricket in life!

Hey… don't go to Google and start searching if such an event happened in the 1980s.

This incident happened recently during the inter-project cricket tournament in Infopro. This incident won't show up in Google until this book gets into the New York Times Best Seller list. But wait, don't lose heart. I will tell you what happened actually.

As you know, we techies are really versatile people. We love sports, arts, movies, Sunny Leone and other beautiful girls. In between, we write some code too. When we get more free time, we try to solve the bugs in the code we wrote earlier. But then, that is strictly based on best-effort basis, after we are done with all activities mentioned above.

HR had come up with the idea of cricket tournament as part of their ESAT improvement initiative. The tournament is now in its 4th year. Each project was asked to put up a team. Each year, the popularity of the tourney was gradually increasing and the fervour reached dizzying heights as the 4th edition unfolded. *Star Sports* tried to get the broadcasting rights of the tourney, but we shooed them away. For us, sport is a very private matter and we don't want the world to watch it and feel envious of us. Now you know why you never got to watch our tournament on any of the channels.

Lives of some of the key players changed forever after each edition of the tourney. Some quit the company because they couldn't handle the failures, some got promotion because their managers were too happy with their scores, and some found girlfriends and some lost their girlfriends.

Dear readers, I know you are eagerly waiting for that turning point in the story. Well, the turning point is the moment when Mr Gavaskar gets selected in our project cricket team.

So, what's so great about that? I can hear you ask this question. Well, I will tell you.

Gavaskar Nair, aka Gavi, hails from Kerala. His father was a great cricket fan. He named his son after the then great Indian player of that time. Later Gavi's father joined the UN and worked in many countries, mostly in Djibouti, Guyana and Senegal. Since Gavi left India immediately after he 'graduated' from Montessori, he never played cricket in school days or saw it on TV. When he was back in India for doing his B. Tech., he somehow never liked the game. His favourite game, as per his CV, was football.

Gavaskar had joined our project this year.

The captain of our project cricket team was Kapil Dev Bansal. He was leading the team since 3 years. He won the cup in the first year and lost out in the first round in the second year. He was given a free hand in selecting his team this year. A few of the slots in the team were filled without selection trials including the people who were known good players. In fact he did not have many in the project. After Suman also quit immediately after latest appraisal, he had in fact lost the last genuine 'inter-project' level player from the team.

Kapil Dev had to include someone from the new joinees and the first name which came to his mind was that of Gavaskar. Thus

Gavi became a part of the privileged default team member group. A few more players were selected through selection trials.

Gavi's troubles started there. Because his name was Gavaskar, people somehow thought he was a good cricket player. Plus, Gavi had kept a cricket ball in his desk (which later turned out to be a memento of his father who was a college player and this was the ball used in a match won by his team). So, his name combined with the ball on his desk, made an impression on others that he was a great cricketer. But, the fact was that he could hardly differentiate a cricket bat from a stump.

Dear reader, by now, you must have understood the kind of deep trouble that Gavaskar had gotten himself into. Rest of the story describes the sorrows and melancholy Gavaskar had to go through because of this irresponsible decision of Kapil Dev. If you are not a mentally strong person, I advise you to stop reading. If you are a very strong person, who can even look at your project manager's eyes and tell him the project issue happened because of his blunder — well, if you are that type of a brave person, please read on.

Tournament was 10 days away. The team started practicing every evening. When he did not turn up for the practice sessions, the captain confronted Gavi.

"I know you are a good player. But if you don't come for practice sessions, we will have to go for someone else. I will remove you from the team," Kapil told him.

"Don't get me wrong Kapil — you should better find a replacement. I don't want to be part of the team."

Kapil was shocked. He had seen people fighting for a place in his team, but, here one guy had outright refused to be part of his team. That was too much.

"Mr Gavaskar, you don't know Kapil Dev well. If I say something, I will do it."

Kapil felt insulted. He took it personally. He thought Gavi did not want to play with him because in last week's review of Gavi's HLD, Kapil had given a lot of comments and Gavi ended up rewriting the whole doc.

'He may be arrogant because he is too good a player,' Kapil thought. 'Hell with his arrogance.' Subsequently, Captain decided to remove Gavaskar from his team.

"But Kapil… we have to somehow win this tournament this year, *yaar*. We need to get Gavi into the team. You have to set aside your ego," Ramu advised him, but Kapil was not ready to listen.

Since the team had lost in the first round last year, there was pressure on Kapil Dev to perform better this time. But, you know, Kapil was a dare devil personality and he does not succumb to such pressures, except when:

"Kapil—*Iss saal mein hum jeetenge na...?*" Sushma asked him during the lunch time.

"Certainly—I have been waiting for this tournament for the last 1 year. This time, the cup is ours," Kapil reassured her. He could see the admiration in her eyes. It was irresistible.

Though he spoke with confidence, in his heart he knew that it was an uphill task to win this time. It was almost like the Indian football captain promising to get the FIFA World Cup in next edition.

Whatever be the case, he had already promised to Sushma. He somehow wanted to win the tournament at any cost. Suddenly, he started feeling the pressure!

"With this team, we can't go very far… I somehow need to get that Gavaskar *saala* in the team," Kapil approached Amrita,

Gavi's batch mate in Infopro to convince him. Kapil knew Gavi had a soft corner for her.

"Gavi—are you not attending the practice sessions…? This time, we need players like you to win the cup for us," Amrita invited Gavi for a coffee and told him in her soft, sexy voice.

"But…"

"No ifs and buts… You should play for the project team. I know you are angry with Kapil because he gave a lot of nasty comments during your HLD review. But you should take it professionally. Take it in your stride."

Gavi cleared his throat. "But… I…"

"No excuses … play for the project team and win the cup… I will give you a treat in the Taj if we go to the second round."

Maan…! An outing with Amrita? Forget about cricket, I am ready to go to space also.

"Someone told me you were the captain of your college team. Have you been part of the university team too…?" she asked.

"Oh… eh … eh… Yes…" Gavi's mind was full of images and moments from the dinner at the Taj which was going to happen in a few days.

"Yes, I used to play for the university." He just uttered those words without thinking too much.

"So you will play for the team…? And … forget the document review comments given by Kapil…?"

"Yes … I will do."

"That is a good boy." She tapped his chubby cheeks softly and left. Gavi could not believe himself. He was not on cloud 9, but in fact cloud 10. His happiness had no boundaries.

If you play cricket for the project team, you get an outing with beautiful Amrita. So, if you play at the national level, what all you can get…? He wondered. "Oh maan… I should have started playing cricket much earlier. I wasted away my time in that hopeless Djibouti and Guyana."

Gavi remained on cloud 10, until he heard the rocking voice of Madhu, his PM. "Hey… Did you complete the status report which I asked you to?" Madhu's voice echoed off the walls of the coffee room. There was a sudden violent quake in cloud 10 and Gavi was thrown out—to the smelly pantry room, stinking with used-tea-bag smell, with an angry PM in front of him (it can't get worse).

"No sir, will send you in another hour."

All through the office hours, his mind was filled with thoughts on how he could give an excellent performance in the cricket tournament.

"Hell … the tournament is starting in 10 days. How do I learn the game in a week and play well?" He started worrying.

"I have performed well in several exams with just 1 night's preparation… I will be able to do this as well." He tried some self-motivation talk.

The reality stared at him like a Project Manager staring at his team member who caused a system shut down. "Oh My God— why did I tell her I was part of the university cricket team? I could have said I have some other program for that week and was not planning to play. Now the only way is to play in the tourney and play well."

He frantically searched for all the websites which gave free cricket lessons and took some printouts.

After office, when he reached his PG accommodation, his roommate Arun was busy watching FTV.

"Arun *yaar*… I am in trouble. I need to learn cricket in the next 1 week."

"Learning cricket…? That too in 1 week…? What's wrong with you?"

Arun was perplexed. Did this guy go mad because of the work pressure? Should I report it to his manager? After one fresher had committed suicide last year, the company had announced incentives for people who reported about their friends who were in mental distress. As Arun was calculating his gross take home for next month including the 'mental-stress-reporting-incentive', Gavi spoke again.

"I need to play for the project team. If the team gets to the second round, I get to go for an outing with Amrita."

"Hey… That's cool… Is the offer valid only for you … or I can also try?"

"You idiot—this is an exclusive offer … not open for public … she likes me because she thinks I am a good cricket player. I just need to take the team to the second round. I need some advice on how to play the different shots and also regarding the different bowling and batting tactics. That's it."

"But… Learning cricket in a week?" Arun did not know what to say. "Maybe you can hire a personal coach," he suggested after a few seconds of thought.

"Why don't you be my coach?" Gavi was quick in smelling an opportunity.

"Me…?" Arun cursed himself for making that suggestion. He knew about Gavi's extraordinary cricketing skills and knowledge. Teaching the circus elephant to play cricket would be much easier. This fat guy couldn't even bend down to pick a ball.

Once when the Indian player Sunil M Gavaskar was appearing on a TV interview, Arun had asked Gavi if he knew who he was.

"Is he a Bollywood actor?"

"No."

"Must be a politician."

"*Saale... yeh bhi nahin jaanta...* This is the Gavaskar who played for Indian cricket team..."

"Is it?" Gavi's eyes widened. He had only heard about the 'other' Gavaskar from his father. He was seeing the person for the first time.

"And now, I have to teach such a dumb guy how to play cricket?" Arun was in total confusion.

Nonetheless, after a few minutes of deliberation, Arun finally decided to take up the task, but for a price.

"Ok agreed... My daily dinner for next week will be on you."

"Agreed."

"Also you have to introduce me to Saniya, your college mate."

"But she is a very good girl..."

"*Saale...* So what...? I am a very good boy too..."

"But you drink and smoke."

"So what? At least I don't spend night out watching FTV, like you."

Gavi felt embarrassed at the last statement.

"Ok — Agreed." He agreed quickly to stop Arun from revealing further secrets.

"Besides, on Saturdays, you should sponsor my pub expenses." Arun put forth the 3rd condition.

Gavi quickly calculated the additional expenses he had to incur for the next 10 days coaching. It was too much for him, but the outing with Amrita weighed higher in comparison.

"Agreed…" After all, there was no other choice if he had to earn a date with Amrita.

"By the way, don't go for the practice sessions with Kapil — just say that you have a customer call or you need to go and attend the CAT classes every evening."

They went out on Arun's bike, bought the cricketing gear, and 2 books, *The Art of Bowling* and *Batting for Dummies*, and the CD of Nagesh Kuknoor movie *Iqbal*. He did a night out to read the 2 books and watch the CD.

"Keep that new abdomen pad in the bathroom. Our bathroom mug is broken. We will use the AP instead," Arun told Gavi who was looking at the Abdomen Pad from different angles and confusing over what was the use of the same.

Practice started in the evening. Arun asked Gavi to throw the ball at him, showed a few stylized shots and asked him to learn his body movements and how to play each shot. After the demo, he started bowling at the trainee. The expectation was that the trainee will emulate each of those bookish shots and clear the ball off the boundary.

Gavi had short sight since childhood. The power of his eyes had changed since the last time he changed his lenses. He could not locate the ball correctly. His bat always went at least 5 inches away from the ball.

"*Abey...* Why can't you connect the bat with the ball? Can't you see the ball properly?" Arun, the coach, was getting irritated after the 20th dot ball of the day in as many balls.

"*Abey...* Don't bowl so fast. It is not an international match. It is only practice," Gavi advised Arun after a 40 kmph volley hit Gavi's nose.

"*Yaar...* That is a wide. A car can pass between the ball and my bat." Gavi had read some Sidhuisms and decided to use it at the opportune time.

At the end of the first practice session the statistics was:

120 balls bowled — 30 declared as wides by the trainee, 60 as too fast and 26 as too slow. 4 balls connected with the bat. In all the 4 cases, the ball went and hit the bat accidentally. Since there were no fielders, one of those hits actually produced a boundary behind the wicket keeper.

The 2 cricket lesson books he purchased the previous day could fetch him only 4 runs in the practice session. So he searched for more 'useful' books. He searched on Google to see if there were any books titled "How to connect the bat with the ball", "100 ways to connect the bat with the ball", "How to see the ball clearly when it approaches crease", "how to avoid getting hit on the nose while playing cricket", etc. He could not find any books.

"There are 100s of other books, but there is nothing for such a simple activity." He lamented. "I should write one next year on that topic."

In parallel, he also searched for information on "what all things to do with a girl on your first outing". He got some suggestions and videos for the last search and was greatly excited!

He found one book titled *Best Shots that will fetch you a Sixer in Every Ball.* He instantly ordered the book from Amazon. His analytic mind did some quick calculations. The book teaches how to hit 6 sixes in an over. Since he is just a beginner, he may be able to adopt only 30% tricks from the book. That will fetch him 2 sixes per over. That is enough for now! He was too happy that someone was kind enough to write such a book.

Next day Arun left early from office and went to the Jumbo Circus in Palace Grounds and took some lessons from the ringmaster. Ring Master explained how to teach a donkey to walk on 2 legs. Arun was happy he got some clues from the session so that he could use them while training Gavi.

That day's practice started little late as Arun took some time to reach the ground from the circus tent. The trainee did not show any signs of improvement that day too. The donkey-teaching-lessons applied by the coach that day also did not work out.

When he came back home in the evening, the book *Best Shots that will fetch you a Sixer in Every Ball* had arrived from Amazon. The book was actually about sales training, nothing to do with cricket.

"You need to be passionate and aggressive on the field. Then only you can take out your full potential in the game." Arun offered another piece of advice. Arun continued "You should learn from our aggressive cricketers such as Sreesanth and Harbhajan Singh."

Gavi took a printout of the photographs of Sreesanth and Harbhajan Singh and hung it on his room wall. He had downloaded the photo from Google Images — it was a photo of both of them standing together. Harbhajan Singh's arms were extended till Sreesanth's nose. Gavi wondered why Sree was standing so near when Harbhajan was bowling. But did not worry about it too much. The caption suggested that the photo was clicked near the 'slap gate' — must be one of the main gates of the Mumbai stadium.

After each day's practice sessions, Arun's hope was fading.

"You should start practicing at home too. Buy a plastic bat and a balloon-sized-bigger plastic ball and practice. Bounce the ball on the wall with your bat."

That was a big morale booster for Gavi as he was able to hit the ball most of the time.

In parallel, bowling practice had also started.

On the 6th day, Arun told him that he was changing the strategy now. Arun asked him to hit the ball which was hung with a string from a bar at the nets. "Try to hit the ball from all angles and you will be a master of all type of shots," Arun advised. "This is how Sachin Tendulkar practices his shots."

Arun had to now spend evenings with Saniya and did not want to "waste time on teaching a 3 legged dumb elephant to climb a coconut tree."

The self-practice trick really worked for Gavi. Unlike on the playground, he could hit the ball in each and every attempt and he was extremely happy about it. Gavi's confidence increased by leaps and bounds.

He thanked Arun for his great advice.

He eagerly awaited their first match of the tourney.

Match Day!

Gavi is included in the playing eleven.

"You did not come for the practice sessions. But I believe you have done your practice well. Do you want to open the innings?" Kapil asked him.

"No... No... Let me bat in the middle order so that I can bat through till the winning run."

The opposite team— 'wireless team'—won the toss and chose batting.

"Would you like to open bowling?" Kapil asked again.

"Not right now. I am focusing on my batting; however I can pitch in with my 'left-arm-leg-break' whenever required. I have practiced a new spin ball 'Tisara'."

"Oh great..." Kapil's confidence only increased after he spoke to Gavi each time.

Though the wireless team made good progress in first 2 overs, they lost some quick wickets and at the end of 6 overs they were 30 for 6.

"We need to finish them off quickly so that we will have a good net run rate," Ramu, the wicket keeper, told Kapil. "That's true," Kapil agreed. "Manu, current batsman, is weak against spin bowling. Let's bring in Gavi from the next over."

7th over. Gavi took to the bowling crease at the Narayana-Tea-Stall-end of the ground. He looked around the ground to ensure that Amrita was present in the crowd. He waved at her, though she did not notice it.

The first ball did not reach the crease. Instead it slipped from Gavi's hand and rushed towards the boundary behind the bowler. Umpire declared a four!

"Boss... Sumit... that can't be considered as a boundary. You don't know the rules," Kapil scolded the umpire.

Sumit, first umpire, got irritated. "Boss, get your facts correct. If the ball goes to the boundary when it is actively in play, it will be declared as a boundary."

"And by the way, the umpire's decision is final."

Kapil was not happy — however he patted Gavi's back and took his field position.

Second ball — it flew from Gavi's hand and went to somewhere in square leg — some 15 metres away from the batting crease. It was like India firing a missile targeting Pakistan, but instead it goes in the direction of South Africa.

Umpire Sumit wondered for a moment whether to give 1 run for that wide or 3 or 4 runs. Sumit had never seen such a 'great wide' in his umpiring life. He noted it in his mind so that he can write about it in his autobiography which he was planning to start soon.

"This pitch is spinning too much," Gavaskar lamented the quality of the pitch and explained the reason for the wide to his captain who was upset with the way the over was going.

Third ball went straight and Manu packed it off to the bushes on the north corner of the ground. Manu cleared the next ball also off the boundary with one bounce.

Gavi was happy that at least his balls were reaching the crease finally. Kapil came near Gavi and gave some advice. "There is a good fielder at 3rd man, give a slow delivery — a slower one slightly on the outside off stump." Gavi did not understand a word of it. He simply nodded his head. Kapil went back happily to the 3rd man, and got ready to take the catch in the next ball.

The next ball was a wide — a full 16 metre distance between the ball and the crease. Umpire checked with the 3rd Umpire Harish if he could give 4 runs for that kind of a wide. Harish called his son at home and asked him to check Wikipedia and call him back.

The next ball was a no-ball cum wide combined. Manu argued that he should be given 2 repeat balls for that wide cum no-ball.

Umpire agreed. One repeat for wide and another one for no-ball. Sumit shouted down Kapil's protest. Sumit was a player last year and Kapil had hit him 3 sixes in an over. So, he does not like Kapil.

Next ball was a no-ball. Then, regarding the next ball, there was a major confusion. Someone said it was the repeat of the previous wide, someone said it was the repeat of the previous no-ball. Someone said it should be the repeat of the current 'no-ball'. The 2 captains quarrelled for 5 minutes. They almost came to blows. Gavi watched innocently from the side. People took his photos and uploaded on 'jokeroftheday.com'. He happily posed for the photos. Umpire Sumit called the 3rd Umpire to give a decision. Harish called his son at home and asked him to check Wikipedia again.

Finally they decided to combine all wides and no-balls into a pool and the repeat ball would minus one number from the pool. If the repeat ball was wide or no-ball, then the count of the pool would increase. This method was suggested by Devender and Lal Singh. So the method was called the DL method. HR took note of the same and decided to report the same to BCCI.

The over went on for 30 minutes. The crowd outside waited anxiously for the climax of the over. 22 wides and 14 no-balls had been bowled in that over. HR person called his friend in BCCI to find out if BCCI would be ready to accept the records being broken in our tournament. The person in BCCI asked for money and HR person cut the call.

After 30 minutes, Kapil forced Sumit to declare that the over was 'over'. There were arguments between the 2 captains and the umpire. They came to blows again. As per Manu, there were 11 more repeat balls left in that over. But finally, when Gavi complained of shoulder pain, people gave it up and agreed to start the next over. So the first time in cricket history, an over was 'declared' just like an innings getting declared.

By this time, wireless team's score had gone from 30 for 6 to 97 for 6.

As Manu had got a good warm up, he continued the onslaught and they scored 147 runs in 20 overs.

After a short break, Kapil and team got ready for the batting.

Kapil and Abdul started the innings.

For a fairly young team, 148 was a huge target. But Kapil was in form. When Mohan got out in the last ball of 15th over, the score was 118 for 4 with Kapil unbeaten on one end. Another 30 runs in 5 overs with 6 wickets in hand looked like a cakewalk. Gavi came in as the next batsman.

Kapil hit the ball to deep midwicket and ran for a single. Gavi started running from the other end. But he had forgotten to take his bat along. It was left in the crease. After he almost reached the other side, he remembered about the bat and so he ran back to get it. He had done that multiple times in his life when he forgot his tiffin box at school.

Kapil thought he was cancelling the run, hence he also ran back. Total confusion prevailed. When the dust got settled, Sumit was standing there with his finger raised. Kapil was out.

It was 118 for 5.

Kapil uttered some words specially to Gavi, but he did not hear it properly. Gavi was happy that he got a chance to bat. He again checked if Amrita was around. He waved his hand. She did not respond.

Ramu joined on the other end.

Gavi used the next 4 balls to study the pace, movement and swing of the ball. So there were no runs. He decided to hit the next ball six. As the ball got released by the bowler, he concentrated all his energy on his wrists and swirled his bat towards the ball. But he had made his shot before the ball arrived. The ball went straight to the keeper. Because of the extraordinary force applied on his wrists, the bat slipped and flew high and away and it went straight towards the batsman on the other side. In 2 seconds, Ramu was lying on the ground with a bleeding head.

By end of over 16, it was 118 for 5 plus 1 retired hurt. There were 4 more wickets to go. 30 runs required from 24 balls.

Subbu came in and he tried to stabilize the innings. He always watched out for what Gavi was doing, so that he did not fall prey like the 2 previous batsmen. As soon as Gavi started moving from his position, Subbu started panicking.

It was last ball of 17th over. Our team at 125 for 6. Subbu's hit went straight into the bowling crease. Gavi was upset that he did not get many balls to bat. When he saw the ball coming towards him, the natural instinct was to hit the ball with his bat. It came slowly rolling towards him and he hit with all his strength. The ball went straight to Subbu's crease and hit the wicket. Subbu was out of crease, ready to go for a single so that he can face next over too.

The bowling team appealed fiercely and from the confused look on the batsmen's face, the Umpire quickly understood that it was better to go with the bowling team's opinion. Subbu was out.

18 balls left. Current score was 125 for 7.

Next batsman, Venky came to the ground with a message for Gavi from the captain. Captain asked Gavi to try for big hits — and that it is ok if he gets out while trying for big shots.

In the next over, Gavi could not properly see the first 3 balls and he could not connect with the next 2 balls. He was clean bowled in the 6th ball. Kapil and his team erupted with joy. At least the biggest threat was gone. But their joy was short lived. Umpire declared it a no-ball. Hence the team got 1 run for the first time when Gavi was standing on the batting crease. Gavi raised his bat towards the crowd and accepted their cheers.

Kapil was heavily disappointed. He came to the ground and argued with the Umpire. He claimed it was not a no-ball and Gavi was out. Opposite team captain argued that Gavi was not out. Umpire Sumit was confused about who belonged to which team. However, he did not budge an inch. Gavi continued in crease.

With great difficulty and utmost care, Venky moved the score board. Every 5 seconds, he would watch out for Gavi's actions to ensure that he was not up to something which would do any harm. He feared for his wicket as well as his life. Ramu was already in St. John's Hospital.

End of 19th over, score reads 140 for 7. Last over started.

Venky hit a boundary and a single in the second and 3rd ball. Now Gavi is at the crease. 3 runs required in 3 balls. As usual, first ball he could not see and second ball he could not connect.

The last ball.

The gallery became silent. People having tea at Narayana Tea Stall stopped talking and all eyes were on the ground. To be precise, all eyes were on Gavi. Gavi's eyes were on Amrita. He ensured Amrita was still around. He waved his hands. She did not respond. His proposed outing with Amrita to the Taj filled his mind. There were just 3 runs—3 silly runs—between him and his dream date with Amrita.

Suddenly something hit his leg. He woke up from his dreams. It was the last ball of the over, which hit below his knee. After hitting his leg with a thud, the ball rolled towards the backward boundary at full speed. As the wicket keeper unsuccessfully chased the ball, bowling team appealed for LBW.

Umpire Sumit's eyes were actually on the snacks being distributed by HR outside the ground. He feared that the snack boxes would be finished by the time he got out of the ground. He had not actually seen how the ball went and he only heard the sound of the ball hitting some hard surface. He assumed it was the sound of the bat hitting the ball. Gavi's legs were straight in front of the wicket, but since the 'ball had hit the bat', Sumit turned down the appeal and a boundary was declared.

Gavi's team had won.

On the gallery, Kapil and friends started dancing and singing.

Gavi sat on the crease. His leg was paining. People who were celebrating did not give him a damn.

Sumit was rushing towards the HR to collect his snacks box. Gavi called him back.

"Can you please press my left leg? The ball was too fast. It is still paining. I can't get up."

"Which one? The last ball?"

"Yes, that one…"

"It did not hit your bat at all???"

"No no… I intentionally was trying to score a leg bye boundary. That was one of my strategies if the bat failed to connect with the ball," Gavi told proudly.

Kapil and team had come running to congratulate the batsmen and they heard the conversation between Gavi and the Umpire.

Sumit immediately called out "Guys ... don't leave... There is small change in the decision about the last ball."

Both teams gathered and stood surrounding Sumit.

"There is a small error—Gavi is actually out. The boundary stands cancelled."

Kapil's team Score is 145 for 8. Wireless team scored 147. So, wireless team wins.

Kapil Dev and his team were out.

Kapil could not control himself. He kicked Gavaskar's ass.

"If you ever play cricket again ... I will kill you," he roared.

Gavaskar was confused and hurt. He was not sure why Kapil beat him for scoring a leg bye boundary.

Next morning, he called Amrita to the coffee room to find out if they could still go ahead with the outing plan as the team had lost by a very slender margin.

People sitting in cubicles besides the coffee room heard the sound of a slap and a shrill cry. They looked around and thought it could be someone beating the street dog outside on the street.

Madhu told me that Gavi has asked for a project change. It seems he wants to move to a unit where there is no cricket tournament. He wants to concentrate on his 'java' skills for now. Sports is secondary.

This Monday, Gavaskar started the process of changing his name in the passport and other documents. He updated his LinkedIn profile with a statement 'I hate cricket. It wastes a lot of time and gives false hopes.'

5: Incredible Interview of Raju

"Man… I can't believe I completed 3 years in Infopro." Raju's eyes widened as he spoke. He was sitting opposite to Amit sipping the tomato soup in the Taj. Amit was going through the menu for the 3rd time, looking to pick the costliest items, as it was a treat from Raju that day.

Raju's mom had found a girl for him — a nurse who was working in Ireland. So, Raju was quitting Infopro and migrating to Ireland after the marriage. Amit insisted that Raju give a treat on the occasion. Raju agreed for the treat, but got an assurance from Amit that he would not tell Subi, Madhu, Prakash and Javed about the treat. The reason he gave was that he wanted to 'control his expenses as he was now entering a more responsible phase of his life'. He told Amit that it would be ok if Aarati, Manjula, Shraddha and Suhana wanted to join, as they very rarely get to go out and eat. But somehow, the plan did not work out and it was only Amit who joined.

"So how did you like the Infopro experience?" Amit asked casually without taking his eyes off the menu. He was ready to listen to Raju only because he was paying. Else, he would have asked him to shut up.

"I enjoyed every moment in Infopro, but you know what, the best moment was the day when I got selected in Infopro. I never got the same level of excitement again in my life," Raju continued. He paused to take another sip of the soup. A smile glowed on his lips.

"When I got selected in Infopro, I felt like I was on top of the world. I was now a Software Engineer, with a compensation of 10,069 INR per month plus 'other emoluments' and free tea and discounted *idli-vada* in the Infopro canteen."

Raju slowly got lost in memories as he continued with his story.

After 12th, he had 'followed the crowd' and joined B. Tech. in one of the leading Engineering Colleges in the South. He somehow managed to pass through the stress and strain of the courses in engineering college for 4 years.

And, finally, he was in the middle of the campus selection week. The week he had been waiting for the last 4 years.

Raju's words flowed almost as if from a radio. It was almost a one way communication. The excitement of narrating one's own life's thrilling moments is an occasion one rarely gets, unless, of course, you are Shah Rukh Khan.

"It was Monday morning 7:30 AM; I as any other engineering student hated Monday mornings. Not only because it is the entry point of reality after the weekend but also because of the first day first show attitude of the day scholars who come with all take home assignments completed and ready for the Prof. to ask just that.

These day scholars don't understand the hardships hostel students go through. Hostel students are too busy with multiple tasks, studies is just a priority 3 task among them. The hard tasks include discussing and debating the agenda for the next week strike (college shut down). The reason for strike could be anything — like the hostel warden stared at the mess secretary or the gate closing time of hostel needed to be extended by 15 minute. They also have to continuously practice playing cards to make the next world rummy champion out of our own college and catch up with the latest Mohanlal movie in the theatre on the first weekend itself, etc. Not to mention about social activities like taking care of the ladies hostel students and making sure the revenue of Madhupoorna (the local bar) is always high. On Fridays, the hostel association even arranges for 'Students-Only' movies. Well, if you wonder what it is, there is a clue—Sunny Leone started her career in such 'students only' movies which teach a lot of Biology to the engineering students who do not have biology in their curriculum otherwise.

But this Monday was even more hated for me as it was the first day of the campus interview.

I lazily got up from the bed and tried to do a flashback of what all hardships I went through in the last couple of weeks to prepare myself for the interviews.

1.	On the evening of the announcement of campus interview itself, I went to town to buy some books for preparation. But, on the way I saw the poster of a new movie in a theatre in the town. Considering the best use of the travel, I decided to get into the movie first (as the movie starts at 6:00 PM and there is no hard and fast entry time for the book shop). The damn movie was 3 hours long. Never knew that there were two disasters in the making. Number one, the movie ended up as a semi art movie. The poster had Mohanlal standing with a big knife. I thought it's for attacking the villains but it turned out that it was for cutting a banana leaf in the movie. The posters are sometime really misleading, you know. Made a mental note that next time I will carefully examine the poster and check for the director's name as well and look for the heroine's face as a back-up plan. Disaster number two was that the book shop keeper was a labour union member and very punctual at closing, though not in opening. He closed the shop at 8:55 (5 minutes he accounts for pulling the shutter and also to fold his lungi and getting ready to leave). Ultimately I ended up borrowing the book from one of the hostel mates.

2.   A CV was asked by the placement unit. I was hearing the word CV for the first time. First I thought it was some medical term like HIV, then someone told me that it is the same as bio-data. I first tried to write a CV correctly and honestly. The name, DOB, Fathers name, Age, Sex, etc., were no brainers. The difficult question came as below:

State a goal in your life. I tried hard to write one. Suddenly, I remembered the way I used to write assignments. Refer to what our seniors have already created. It's not considered a good thing to re-invent the wheels, not only in the corporate world, but also in the academic world. From some seniors' CVs and my peer CVs, I managed to do some mix and match and write my life goal as below (combining the better produces the best).

'I am an extraordinary hardworking, ambitiously forward looking and determinedly target oriented person. Wherever and Whatever I work, I try to bring it to the perfection on schedule, on time and with great quality.'

I thought for a moment if I should be very frank and state that my most interesting time pass is to check out the girls in the institute, but decided to keep some of these secrets for my autobiography and leave them alone while preparing the CV. Since I couldn't think any better hobby than watching TV, I also flicked the hobbies list from the best of CVs like writing, instrumental music, etc.

Finally, a few days before the interview, I and a few of my classmates decided to do a combined study. The 'study' started at 7:00 PM. For 30 minutes, we discussed on how to go about the combined study. Once we decided on the mode of operation, someone suggested taking a 'short' break to play cards and start the combined study at sharp '9:00 PM'. The 'short' break got more and more interesting and it became slightly longer — till 5:00 AM in the morning. None of us actually 'got time' to meet again afterwards.

And, to end with, last night I tried to do some aptitude test. After crawling my way through a few problems, my eyes fell on the latest issue of *Filmfare* magazine. Kareena Kapoor smiled to me from the cover and that was the end of the preparations.

Day 1 of campus interview: India's No 1 software company (which makes vehicles, steel, etc., as well)

I thought I did well in the aptitude test. The next is what they called Psychometric test. I assumed it was named after the guy who composed the questions. The question paper looked normal at first, the initial questions were somewhat like those given below:

Q1. In a team, you like to

a)   lead

b)   listen

c)   participate

d)   fight

What a simple question, of course lead.

Q2. In a team, you will

a)   listen to all

b)   don't listen to anyone

c)   listen to a few

d)   don't listen to few

Another simple one. Answer to question 1 clearly states you are a lead — if you are a lead then, of course, you need not have to listen to anyone…

There were almost 100 or so questions like this and there were only 30 minutes. Soon, I found that some of the questions were repeating.

Bloody hell!!! I thought only university question papers are wrong, how come campus interview question papers have mistakes??? I was furious at the callousness of the guys who prepared the question paper.

I knew what to do in such situations. Just attempt the questions. It doesn't matter whether the answer is right or wrong, all people who attempted will get marks. My mother had taught me this trick while preparing for the 10th class exam. I follow that too up to the last bit even now. Once I identified the trick, it was all easy… The remaining 68 questions were answered in 9 minutes flat.

At 2:00 PM, the shortlisted candidate list came. Surely there is some mistake. My name was not there. Is there a revaluation procedure for campus interview tests?

Met Satish in the corridor.

"Raju, I am sure your name is in the top of the list." Satish had a very satisfactory smile on his face.

I felt like hitting him on his head. Surely this guy had seen the list and wanted to apply some chilli to my wound.

I told, "You know there is an upper cut off for this company. They know that the people who clear the upper cut offs will go for IIMs. So they won't take the people who clear the upper cut off. It looks like I cleared the upper cut off. I had actually made an intentional attempt to score less and come within the cut off. Don't know how this happened. I am sure your name is in the list." And that was a hard hit on Satish's head.

Satish's smile disappeared. Before he met me, he was overjoyed that he was in the list and I was not. But now, he started worrying that he did not make the cut off for 'IIM' and I did. IIM was his life dream!

'Maybe you can try for a re-evaluation,' I told kindly. 'If you find the procedure for re-valuation, let me also know — that Suresh also was asking for the procedure.'

Satish was almost fainting. He went into depression and rushed to enquire about the re-evaluation procedure for the campus interview. He couldn't believe that he did not make the IIM cut off.

Days passed, the first seven companies passed without even winking at me.

I decided to try a different tactic. Next aptitude test, instead of trying to find answers, I just marked some random answers in the MCQ.

I did not have much hope. As I was about to take the auto to the Madhupoorna to find some solace, someone came running to inform me that I was short listed.

I asked, 'Are you sure it is my name — Raju Mathews? Is it my name or is it that of that 'Mech' guy Raju Velayudhan — he also has not got a job till now.'

'No, I am sure it is you.'

I was disappointed at losing a session in the bar, but at least when I call home in the evening, there is some cheering news for mom.

And the result announcement unravelled a miracle. I too was shortlisted.

Miracles have happened multiple times in history. It happened in Jesus Christ's time! It happened in Moses' time. And now a miracle has happened in my time too.

I was actually shocked. By that time, the recruitment representative came and informed me that there will be 3 people in the panel. One HR, one technical person and third is a Personality Assessment Specialist. Maan… are they recruiting engineers or CEOs directly???

I had to borrow formals from my roommate as the available ones were in the bin, waiting for the dhobi to come and collect. The dhobi was busy washing the suits and ties for the people who had been going through multiple rounds of interviews. And poor guys like me were ignored by the dhobi since last week. We had to put up with the stinking smell in the rooms and the hidden worries in our hearts.

I was already uncomfortable from not wearing my own dress and shoes. Plus, the news of having 3 experts in the panel sent a shudder through my body. With shivering body, I entered the interview room.

There was one younger looking guy in jeans and T-shirt, another HR type guy in semi-formals and a third very stern looking guy.

I tried to remember the advices from *Competition Success Review* magazine, usually written by IAS toppers on how to face interviews. Realized soon, it's easy to write after interview, not so easy to do it on the fly. My throat was drying. God save me … this is my first job interview in life…

'My mom is already tense that I will go jobless and will have to go to the Gulf and work in some oil mines. I badly want to clear this.'

After formal wishes, they offered me a seat. I slowly kept my file on the table and placed my hands on top of the table (*Competition Success Review* says, you shouldn't hide your hands). All this time, the stern looking guy was following me like a camera.

When I placed my hands on top of the table, he started staring at the hands. This is strange. What's wrong with this guy? I haven't even stared at a girl like this. My shivering increased.

'Maybe he just noticed that I have not cut my nails for the past 3 months. Oh God — Now I know why my mom always used to insist on keeping my nails clipped and clean.'

To avoid further disaster, I neglected *Competition Success Review*'s advice and pulled my hand down.

The young looking technical guy started his missile of questions. He was like a computer programmed to ask 1 question in every second. Fifty percent of the time, my eyes were on the stern looking guy and his eyes were 100% time on my movements. I was in the same situation like an Indian cricketer batting in a West Indian pitch with Walsh and Ambrose bowling at two ends.

'What do you think about the latest technology trends?' The technical member of the panel started.

Oh God , that's a googly. I had never thought about any technology trends. Why should I? There is not even enough time to think about my assignments, preparation for world rummy championship, sessions in the local bar and of course about the sweet girls in my class. Now this guy is asking about something which I never even thought about in my dreams. Now what do I say. Can I say 'pass' or is there a 'phone a friend option'?

'Well ... sir... Technology trends ... Sir ... they are very good Sir...' I started with a stammering, but picked up speed as I laboriously picked each word from the deepness of my stomach and somehow made it come out through the mouth. 'My friends and I always talk about it in our hostel rooms ... sometime even in college bus we talk about it Sir... Technology trends are very very good sir.'

'Why do you think it is good?'

'Well sir … it is not about what I think or you think … Sir. Technology trends are always good. Even George Bush made a statement about this while visiting Oxford campus last week sir…

Did you read about it in *Competition Success Review* Sir?' I posed a reverse question.

The interviewer was stumped. He had not read the *CSR*, in fact the only magazine he had read after getting his Infopro job was *Filmfare* and this particular news on technology trends was never reported in *Filmfare*.

To avoid further uncomfortable reverse questions from the interviewee, the interviewer changed the topic and went on to another question.

'What do you think about mobility?'

Other than for sending SMS to girls and for watching hot clips, I had never thought of any other use for the mobile. But I didn't want to get caught for this question. I remembered all the ads in TV regarding mobiles and answered,

'Mobility connects people, it follows wherever you go and its about applications' and finally I decided to add the master stroke world 'cloud' as well into it.

The computer-programmed-interviewer continued his onslaught with many of those silly 'out-of-syllabus' questions. I felt like an English batsman facing the bodyline series. I somehow defended most of them on front foot and somehow avoided a direct hit on my wicket. However, in the process, some of the 'volleys' really hit my nose and I bled profusely as well.

By the time the minute hand of the room clock ticked away a full half circle, I was at my wits end. The 30 minutes looked like eternity to me. To hell with these bloody Dinosaurs and their interview. If I leave now, I still have time to catch up with my friends in the bar. I just wanted to leave the room.

And the Dinosaurs fired the final Yorker at me. 'Why do you need this job?'

I was already fed up with the whole process, so I could not completely control my emotions. 'It's not me who need this job, it's you who are trying to recruit me.'

And I started packing my file folder and other belongings.

The computer-programmed-interviewer was hugely impressed. Never in his life, any interviewee had answered his question with so much confidence and authority. Before he was leaving for the interview sessions from Infopro, his boss had told him to pick smart, confident, brave candidates who can confidently face the customer and provide leadership to the delivery teams. It seems Infopro believes in smart people than good people.

His eyes glittered like a would-be groom who finally found a matching bride after wading through so many profiles in the bharatmatrimony.com.

And, then to my surprise, the Psycho man spoke.

'Mr Raju you have passed our stress test. We were looking for a product selling person and we wanted someone who can give smart answers than a person with right answers. A person who is fearless in facing the customer and can stand his ground and make the customer understand the value of the product. You have made it!!!'

That was a surprise. I had thought that after the interview, the psycho might scold me for not cutting my nails for past 3 months or even hit me with the scale in his hand.

I couldn't believe my ears. Instead of Dinosaurs in front now I saw angels in the interview panel. Kareena Kapoor in the film magazine was smiling at me.

As I walked past the interview room door, Satish came running to me to ask what the panel asked, as he was to get in after half an hour.

With a cupid smile, I replied — 'Boss … these guys are hardcore techies… Get your fundas correct… Refresh your S5 Electronics Circuits. Do you remember the process of making a diode in the factory ? The top 10 industrial uses of astable multi-vibrators? Name of the person who invented Cathode Ray Tube?'

Satish panicked big time. He could not recall answers to any of those questions. He almost fainted.

As Satish ran to his room to search for the S5 text books, I waited for an auto to take me to the Madhupoorna bar to join my friends."

"So exciting!" Amit's words woke up Raju from his memories.

Amit's eyes were on the chicken breast served just a minute back by the waiter. Raju could not make out if Amit was commenting about his story or about the chicken.

When the bill arrived, he realized that he had missed many important things happening at his own table when he got lost in his memories. Bill was coming close to 10K. Half month salary gone. Until now, Raju was only sure about the highest point in his Infopro journey. Now he knew that he was just at the lowest point.

6: Infopro way of aligning to Customer mindshare

It was a Wednesday morning. Things were normal till 10:30 AM. That is when Ramesh Srinivasan, my manager came to my cubicle and asked me to look at the mail he just forwarded to me.

Wednesdays are particularly boring days of the week. First of all the weekend is still 2 days away. There are no project meetings on Wednesday. Project meetings are usually interesting in many ways. You could hear the best of imaginations as reasons for not meeting the deadlines. In last week's meeting, Lalitha's reason for not meeting the deadline was computer keyboard was slow while Suresh had to take part in 'Mr IT' competition conducted by the Fitness Freak Gym and Rimi's in-laws wanted her to be back home by 5:00 PM.

Working in finance domain for long had somewhat made my work monotonous. Though I am by designation Technical Architect, there is nothing much to "architect" in many of the projects. Most of the financial firms have similar data base and security requirements. So, I ended up in re-using the same set of design principles. I even got an award from KM team this year as the best practitioner in IT-reusability.

As usual, today morning also I went through the *Times of India* (TOI) *Ascent* supplement, and found that there are a lot of opportunities in Telecom and networking and none for finance.

'Maan … these Telecom folks are lucky … they are always in demand…' I thought. Post the *TOI* review, I caught the bus to office, picked up one CCD coffee on the way and walked straight to the cubicle. I was about to switch on the machine, that's when Ramesh walked in.

"Biju, we have just received another exciting lead. We may not have done anything similar before, but from my initial analysis, I am sure you can crack it," Ramesh told.

"Check the mail I just forwarded." He added.

By this time my machine had started booting up. My laptop is 6 years old. Due to its age and the wear and tear, the machine has become so lethargic that it takes anywhere from 15 to 20 minutes to boot up. Usually, I enter the cubicle, switch on the machine and go to the next cubicle and chat with Ms Aparna Mishra, until the laptop comes up. I consider those 20 minutes of booting time as my best time in office. I am also trying out some ways if I can increase the booting time by another 5 or 10 minutes so that I can use my time in more appropriate and enjoyable ways.

But today Ramesh has spoiled my daily routine.

Meanwhile, my machine has slowly started showing up signs of coming to life. I could hear some strange sounds, huffing and puffing noises from inside the laptop. Poor guy is really sweating it out to somehow come up and be ready to accept all the junk I would be typing-in during the day. First, the desktop security sign-in prompt came. In an attempt to hide my password (which was the name of one of the girls in the project) and type fast, I typed it wrong twice and Windows showed the warning that the password will be locked if one more attempt is wrong. To avoid the whole process of raising a service request, calling the ever un-answered extensions of the computer department multiple times and then finally walking to their building (which is 1 kilometre away and across the highway), I decided to type the password slowly even if that makes Ramesh see that. Luckily Ramesh himself was looking at the next cubicle new joinee girl and I could type my password slowly but correctly.

Subsequently, the laptop opened many screens at a time like a magician. The Window's login prompt, power manager shut off prompt screen, HRDs KIOSK of the day screen and computer department's tip of the day screen came up. I customarily closed them. Next turn was of the firewall update window, Adobe install window and the Java update window. Just like the previous screens, I put them also to sleep. Next in the daily custom was to kill the hourly activity tracking window screen and the process. Finally, I got a somewhat clean window. There were still some computer updates blinking in the taskbar. I avoided them as they were per se not disturbing my visual of the working window.

"*Aree* Boss… *Kya ho raha hai…*?" The girl in the next cubicle just left her seat and so now Ramesh's eyes had again fallen back on me.

Since Ramesh was losing his patience, I tried to open the Outlook mail box first. Otherwise my usual routine was to open MSN India and read the headlines and if possible discuss the movie news with Aparna. At the same time, I clicked the Outlook mail box, the messenger also tried to get auto open and then there was a tussle between two Microsoft applications to the get the CPU time. In the war of the CPU cycles, Outlook somehow won and started opening. The Outlook opened with a red bar at the top saying "Mailbox full, you have exceeded the limit of 100 MB". I usually keep my mailbox clean at least to 5 MBs. Soon I identified the culprit. Ramesh had forwarded a mail with some huge attachment. Ramesh was vigorously pointing at the same. I opened the mail which looked somewhat like below:

From: Ramesh Srinivas

Sent: Friday, June 6, 2014 9:52 AM

To: Biju Kumar

Cc: Suresh Gupta; Kishore Singh

Subject: FW: Meeting Today with Packet Systems

Fyi

From: Suresh Gupta

Sent: Friday, June 6, 2014 9:51 AM

To: Ramesh Srinivas

Cc:

Subject: FW: Meeting Today with Packet Systems

fy

From: Kishore Singh

Sent: Friday, June 6, 2014 9:50 AM

To: Suresh Gupta

Cc:

Subject: FW: Meeting Today with Packet Systems

FYI

From: Ram Murthy

Sent: Friday, June 6, 2014 9:49 ARE

To: Kishore Singh

Cc: Rahul Gupta; Hemanth Vora

Subject: FW: Meeting Today with Packet Systems

Kishore,

Looks like this belongs to your delivery unit. Attaching the latest PPT template and some collaterals.

Ram

From: Hemanth Vora

Sent: Friday, June 6, 2014 9:44 AM

To: Ram Murthy

Cc: Rahul Gupta

Subject: Meeting Today with Packet Systems

Ram,

Customer was very vocal about ATM in the call, let us pitch that strongly. Let's give the presentation by this Monday. That will help us to book the order in this quarter itself! Quickly went through one of the old Wall Street Journals. ATM market in US could touch 25 billion by 2010.

Regards,

Hemanth

I finished reading the mail quickly.

Ramesh started explaining the context "Biju, Since I know that you have some cycles, I want you to look at this proactive pitch. Customer is visiting us next Monday. The sales folks are very excited about this opportunity. See the mail has come from our department sales head, Hemanth directly. By looking at the business value at stake, I am sure we are just in front of the biggest opportunity of the decade."

"But there is no useful information in this mail which will help me to prepare the solution" My genuine doubt!!!

"Biju, didn't you hear our unit head talking last week, we need to develop our threads more. In business, you won't get everything in black and white. See, there is a word ATM in the mail. And we know the ins and outs of ATM. Whatever service they need regarding ATM, we will give it. I am sure you can develop on that. What I gather is that our competitors do not know about this yet."

"But, the sales people are not talking about what the customer really wants. Isn't that what Sales is supposed to do?" I argued further.

"See Biju, don't waste your time in asking too many silly questions. I cannot ask our Sales head now what the customer wants. If I ask, he will tell that we are supposed to know that as we belong to delivery. Instead, it is best we work on what information we have and come up with the slide pack. I will review it and we will correct it together. BTW, you will be presenting this to the customer as well on Monday."

I immediately knew rest of my week and obviously the weekend was also gone. From the single word of ATM in the slide, I have to now make the whole slide pack.

Ramesh put the final nail in the coffin, "Biju, you know I will be very busy this weekend and mostly will be taking Friday off as well. So, I have told the Sales people to include you in all the calls as well..."

Traitor, you left me alone in the battle field!!! I felt as if I am standing between the India–Pakistan border with firing going on between them.

Soon, Ramesh left and like Sherlock Homes I started going through the mail chain to find any trace of useful information. The mail had come from the top of the sales, flown down to the bottom of the sales and then gone to the top of the delivery and finally reached me without any value-add in between. My "delivery leadership" had added only 3 "fyi" headers in the process. And that too one 'leader' has typed only 2 letters 'F Y'. I wondered if that was inadvertent or did he include it as the short form for the Hollywood films' favourite abusive word.

I checked the attached slides. One was a template slide explaining the font, colour, etc., to be used and the second one was a huge attachment of 100 slides with case studies of every damn project executed in the unit (a 15 MB bazooka!!!)

I downloaded the bazooka and kept it in a folder, then moved the mail to a local folder to release the stress of mail box.

By this time, 3 sets of calendar invites came to me whose titles read as below,

9:00 AM–11:00 AM–Brain storming, On Call

1:00 PM–2:30 PM–Sync up, On call

9:00 PM–11:00 PM–Deck review, On call

All these were daily calls for next 5 days including weekends. This confirmed that next 5 days of my life were going to be wasted.

Another mail also came, saying Kick Off call which was slated at 11:00 AM today was in the next 5 minutes. Given a choice, I would like to Kick off these folks who waste others' time in numerous calls—brainstorm, kick off, synch up, review, re-review, leadership review, management review, steering committee meeting and what not. Just like the 'Ad' for *Agarbattis*, everybody has a 'reason' to call for a meeting.

I quickly went to the washroom. Came back and dialled into the call. After 3 attempts which resulted in "line busy", "you are in queue" and "currently unavailable", the VOIP bridge finally dialled me in. The lady's voice in the bridge told I was the 6th caller. I immediately realized that the war zone was ready and at least 5 valiant warriors were out on the field with their arms and ammunition.

The moment my "ting" tone was heard, the bridge erupted. "Biju, we were waiting for you." I made mental notes '...In the sense, the butcher is waiting for the goat to be cut...'

Since I didn't find any conversation useful, I started writing down the "Key words" in the conversation. Below are the "most used words" winners. Value Proposition (27 times), Cost advantage (22 times), Offshoring (lost count after 40), domain knowledge (20 times), Competition (15 times), End to End (17 times), USP (20 times), winning strategy (23 times), differentiator (31 times).

After many rounds of discussion the sales and delivery agreed upon the following TOC for the presentation:

1.	Our Company & History

2.	Our clients

3.	Our vision

4.	Our focus areas

5.	Our Units

6.	We know everything about ATM

(It was decided to take a picture of a real ATM machine and mark all the parts of it and show that we had worked on all of it. When I mentioned that we have probably only software skills, the sales immediately cut me off and asked zone to get my ATM basics correct. As in, all of us take money from ATM machines and we that way can claim 'hands on' experience with ATM machine hardware as well.)

7.   Our offerings and services in ATM space

(There was a huge discussion on whether the money changing in the ATM is a service to be included or not. Sales insisted that it needs to be included as "Professional Service" and that way we can show more than 1 Lakh professionals against that skill in our company as anybody including the washroom napkin change guy can do that work.)

8.   Case studies

(I told there is no hardware related case studies. Then I was asked to Google and find few keywords and make a few 'compelling' case studies).

One of the attendees suggested that he had heard from one of his LinkedIn friend's Facebook friend working in Ethiopia, that our company had done some great work for a Somalian company in the 1980s. That would be a great differentiator. He said. Just enquire about it and get that case study.)

9.   Value we can deliver—Sales insisted that no "usual suspects" value adds should be missing and all of them should be saying more than 25% improvement year on year.

After a few minutes, I got a MOM mail with most of the above sections assigned against me. It confirmed my fate for the next few days.

By evening that day, I sent a PPT Packets_Presentation_v.01 to all the meeting participants. The very next day I realized the danger of sending a PPT very early in the cycle. The whole sales force in the US and India had commented on the slides. There were different forms of comments like, embedded comments in the slides, detailed comments in the email, comments added as notes, etc., etc. One MBA guy who newly joined the sales team even prepared another slide deck including all the comments he had on my deck. His 'comments deck' had 20 slides more than my original presentation.

'This guy should definitely be from an IIM,' I thought. Later I confirmed the same from his LinkedIn profile.

The comments I got ranged from colour and angle of arrows in the diagram to all the way of changing the whole structure of the slide.

Later in the day, the set of calendar meetings started. The sales people were like Virender Sehwag in his heydays batting, no mercy on me. The verbal comments were flying thick and fast in the air like sixes and fours. Whenever I tried to defend some points, they called a no-ball. One sales guy felt that the slide didn't make any 'impact', while other felt that value proposition was not coming out. Another one felt it should be more 'seductive'. 'Ok—maybe we will ask Rakhi Sawant to prepare the PPT'—I thought.

A fourth guy wanted all the fonts to be changed to Calibri and font size to 10.853. It seems he had used the above font in another presentation and he had won that deal. I collected all the comments and started working on the same.

My next few days went in making and re-making the slide ware. The versions of the slide went from v.01 to v.21 in two days. Just like an empty plot on a Bangalore roadside which is used by the neighbours to dump waste and by the pedestrians to urinate, every one of the sales guys who heard about my review meetings, jumped onto the meeting and excreted their intellectual waste on my slide deck.

After every review I had to 'clean' my slide deck. Just before the weekend, I sent the presentation to the sales head Hemanth Vora. To give an indirect message that I was not going to make any more changes in the slide, I named the slide deck as Packets_Presentation_Final. Next day morning I got the reply from Hemanth with a single line as below:

"The story line is not tight. It does not have the punch."

I tried to find any clues from the slide or the mail what that comment meant, but Mr Vora had not left any clues. I had heard of story-lines in the context of movies. Never thought a PPT should have one. Decided to ask what that meant in the weekend morning meeting.

Saturday morning meeting started with a note that Hemanth was not very happy with the slide and wanted the storyline to be changed. I asked innocently what was wrong with the new storyline. The answer from the sales was that there is not enough 'WOW' factor in the slide.

"What is the WOW factor?" I asked.

"You know, it does not have the required punch. The slides are not appealing."

Then the sales person gave a 30 minutes lecture of which I didn't understand a single word. Sales wanted to have a dry run that evening. I told them that I have to go and buy a new suit for the presentation that evening and they agreed. Finally dry run was set for Sunday morning.

Sunday morning dry run was attended by Hemanth as well. He asked me to present as-if in-front of the customer. I tried my level best. Hemanth exclaimed that I sounded as if I had not had enough breakfast. I asked how it could be presented better. Hemanth 'immediately' remembered about another 'important' call he had to attend and dropped off the call at once before I could repeat my question. Other sales guys in the call asked me to prepare by practicing in front of the mirror.

The D-Day came, Monday morning. I was already uncomfortable as the sales folks told me to wear a suit. It was the end of April and the south Indian sun had no mercy. While coming out of the house my maid gave me a look as if I was wearing a swimming outfit. A few autos that I waved to didn't stop thinking that I was some income tax officer. Finally I got into a Volvo bus, the bus conductor and driver thought I was a TTR and told me that the bus wouldn't go to the railway station. After the morning hurdles, somehow I reached office before the stipulated time.

The customer came on time. After the initial meet and greet, the presentation started. The customer looked bored with the long story about the company. There was as small section on telecom and networking. Customer started asking some questions in the section. To vent my frustration on telecom folks, I added telecom and networking as a de-focused area in our company. I was wondering why this customer was interested in telecom. Then I thought nothing unusual in that, nowadays it's fashionable for any customer to ask something about networking as it's the bleeding edge. My account manager presented the finance unit credentials. Customer didn't seem to be particularly interested.

Finally my section started. Sales guys gave an intro saying that the ATM expert from the company is presenting. Sales guy took some full 5 minutes to introduce myself as someone who had been associated with ATMs since my birth. He even went to the extent of saying my father and grandfather also worked on ATMs. I was getting some of my new lessons in how to sell.

The customer looked at me hopefully with widened eyes. My first slide was the ATM machine photograph slide (for originality one of the sales person had taken the photograph of an ATM machine near his house). The customer looked puzzled. I continued the presentation. With every slide, the customer seems to get worried and frustrated. From the customer's facial expression, Hemanth thought he wanted to go to the loo urgently and he kindly pointed the customer in the direction of the toilet.

And with that, the customer was more irritated.

Finally, he told us to stop and he asked "Do you guys understand ATM?" Sales folks looked double confused.

"Of course—we, in Infopro understand the ins and outs of ATMs. We have been servicing multiple fortune 500 customers on ATMs and even BTMs for the last 15 years. And we at Infopro..."

"Would you please stop?" customer interrupted.

Nobody knew what to do.

Hemanth tapped Arjun's shoulder. "Hey... Looks like he does not like ATM presentation. You have the other 'cloud' wallah slide deck, right. You present it now. We should hook him up on one of these topics."

"Hey... But he never asked for Cloud presentation," I protested.

"No need to ask." All IT companies in India give 'cloud' presentation irrespective of whoever is visiting the company. We can also do. No harm.

Finally account manager called customer to next room where refreshments were kept. Gave him a glass of butter milk so that his inside would cool down a bit. Through the glass door we could see the animated discussion between the two.

The customer told the AM that we were morons and didn't understand anything about technology. He was cutting short his visit and leaving. The customer left in a hurry and he even forgot to return his temporary pass at the gate. The security guard tried to run behind the car but in vain.

There was detailed root-cause analysis and de-brief meeting. Sales tried to pin the blame on delivery — that the presentation from delivery didn't have enough meat, sufficient punch, necessary oomph and the required WOW factor. I told the slides were reviewed multiple times and all the comments were taken care of and every inch of the slide was talking about ATM. The sales also felt something else was wrong, no one could find what the cause was.

After the disastrous presentation and de-brief, I went to my desk. One of the first things I tried was to open the website of the customer company. The website had the information about all the technologies they work with and in one of the pages the expansion of ATM was there — It read Asynchronous Transfer Mode (the communication protocol) and not Automatic Teller Machine.

I did not want to reveal the truth. If I revealed it, I would end up sitting at my desk on the weekend and preparing the next presentation on Asynchronous Transfer Mode.

7: Post Appraisal Tremors

Infopro is a 'cool' company! That is what our ads in *Times of India Ascent* claims. That is true as far as the customer deadlines are concerned, as we are really very 'cold' towards them. The only time when the campus atmosphere gets heated up is during our 'Appraisal Season'. During the appraisal time, we shed our tag of 'cool' company for a month. The temperature soars. And there is fire, lightning and even miniature volcanic eruptions all around.

People fight with their managers and second level supervisors. We invent fictitious reasons why some of our peers got better rating than us. People shout at the security when he asks for the ID card or at the waiter at the cafeteria for the change in colour of the *sambar*. All these are symptoms of 'appraisal season'.

The coffee rooms are the places where the emotions get a vent. People bad mouth their managers, and sometimes, they badmouth the people who did the 'design' and 'development' of the manager — his parents.

As you walk in front of the conference rooms where the feedback discussion happens, you get to hear voices of various emotions — sometimes angry shouts, sometimes sad sobs, sometimes pleading and begging and sometimes even sounds of slaps being exchanged.

Well, this story is about one of those miniature volcanic eruptions!

Appraisal season was at its peak.

Last 2 years, salary hike was withheld due to various reasons like the 'thunderstorm in California', 'snowstorm in Europe', 'El Nino in Peru' and the increased activity of 'Somalian pirates in the Arabian Sea'.

We were expecting some hike this year.

I had my appraisal feedback discussion just completed.

Most of my tasks were rated as 'Average' or 'Below Average'. My coding was average, design was below average. If my design is below average, how can I write 'average' code based on that? I wanted to ask Sharan, my manager. But he may bring down the rating for coding also to below average. So I kept quiet.

My code review skills 'Needed Improvement' and my 'client relationship building capability' was 'Non Existing'.

Sharan told me that I was not living up to the role expectations. In my feedback sheet, he listed each and every mistake, major and minor sins from last year, some of which I could not even recollect.

"Sir, please don't include this load build break I caused—this appraisal period is up to March 31st. The load break happened on April 1st."

"You know what—our customer is in the US and we work according to the US time. You caused this load break in the morning 10:00 AM, which was 11:30 PM on March 31st in US."

I cursed myself for coming early for work that day. I should have come after each one of those bloody US clocks went past midnight.

Sharan actually keeps a diary to note down the mistakes committed by each of his team members. He even writes the timestamp of the crime, just like an FIR. And he uses this 'Case

Diary' at the time of appraisal. So even if you don't remember your mistakes, he will surely do. I am afraid he will send the diary to god when one of us dies. Then I will end up in hell for sure, because god will get to know of all my sins from the diary.

Someone told that Sharan had got the idea for this diary from his wife. It seems his wife keeps track of all his wrongdoings. She does not even use a diary, but her mind is her notepad.

"Sir, what about these 3 P1 bugs in a week Sir? It was done by my reportee Ramu. Please don't punish me for that," I pleaded.

"Boss, you are responsible for what your reportee did. If your subordinate is not good, you should have done that work yourself."

Then he repeated that statement again—I don't know why.

Then he said "No innovations done during the year."

"Sir, during the customer visit in December, when our Automatic Voice Response was not working, I was the one who suggested getting 2 SEs to hide behind the PBX and work as a temporary AVR for customer demo purpose. Isn't that innovation?"

"Boss... you should have got the AVR working properly. You put a Bengali and Mallu behind the PBX. Those guys spoke with heavy accent. We somehow escaped. That was a 'dirty' workaround, not an innovation."

Bull shit—this same guy had appreciated me then, for saving the customer demo somehow. Now he is saying it was cheap—Useless guy.

He had written 'Not eligible for promotion' in the recommendations box. I knew he was going to prefer Rukma, the beautiful girl who joined 6 months back from our competitor. She is 3 years junior to me.

"Sir... I have already completed 4 years in this role Sir... All my friends have gone to the next level," I pleaded.

I pushed his pen from the table as I spoke. As he bent down to pick up the pen, I sprayed a bit of glycerine in my eyes. When he came back up, I had tears flowing down my cheeks.

He offered me his towel, then withdrew it and offered me the last page of my appraisal printout, to wipe my tears. The printed letters on the 'recommendation box' got erased with my tears.

But my tears went waste. He did not budge on the appraisal ratings and comments.

Bastard... He was so upset when one of the girls in the project cried because she split with her boyfriend. He even took her to the Coffee Cafe Day. But this bloody guy does not care even 1% about my tears! I thought for a moment if I could push a complaint to HR under the 'gender bias' category.

"Boss... How can I make you the PM? People don't even listen to you. You can't control people. I have assigned you one guy — Ramu — as your reportee. I will observe you for a year more and see how you are managing your 1 member team. Then we can talk about it."

"And project managers don't cry like this. You need to be a tough guy." He advised.

It was news to me that project managers don't cry. Just 2 weeks back, I had seen the PM Santosh being beaten up by his Facebook girlfriend's brothers, right in Silk Board junction. He was crying loudly. Isn't he a PM? Anyway, I did not want to argue with Sharan — he will screw up my next year appraisal also. The moment he completes the appraisal discussion, he starts a new page in his diary for the sins of next year. So I need to be careful.

My tears and the 100 Rupees I spent on the glycerine bottle went down the drain — a total waste. It was Ranjit Sivaraman who had suggested this idea to me. He said his wife had tried this in ABC Consulting and it had worked. Waste fellow. I should claim the money from him.

As I walked out of the room, wiping my eyes, I saw Chinthu, the HR guy.

I asked him if there was a chance for me to get promoted to the PM level since I had completed 4 years in the current role. He said there was no vacancy; I would get a promotion only if Sharan moved out. I was disappointed. I didn't see any reason why this monkey would move out in the near future.

So my appraisal was put to rest. As usual, my Manager had concluded that I was a hopeless guy wandering around in the wrong place. I am sure he would have given 'exceeded expectations' to Rukma. To be frank, when I heard that a girl was joining our team, I did not have much expectation. But when I saw Rukma, Gosh...! I knew she had 'Exceeded Expectations'. So I can't blame Sharan for that rating, perhaps.

Appraisal discussion was ending on Friday, in next 4 days. I still had to complete the feedback session for Ramaswamy, my only reportee.

Ramu just had 2+ years' experience. Ramu was in another project and had got poor ratings in his last year appraisal. He started crying loudly when he got the ratings last year. He cried sitting in his cubicle and lamented how a top ranking guy from the St. Mary's Convent School like him was rated so poorly.

Someone complained to HR that his crying sound was horrible and disturbing and it was delaying their project deliverables! Someone from the other wing came running thinking that a dog had been trapped in a window in our wing. They went back when they saw it was not a dog but a donkey-headed engineer.

HR swung into action quickly and took him to the HR bay and tried to pacify him. He continued crying in the HR bay as well. HR folks also got irritated. They frantically searched in the policy repository, if there was any company policy to 'fire someone with immediate effect for crying aloud and causing project delays'! Though they searched for half an hour, they could not find any relevant policy to be invoked, so the HR manager sent a note to the HR head asking him to add this special amendment while revising the policy in the coming year.

He asked for a project change and after a lot of discussions, cry marathons, etc., he was asked to report to Sharan for the subsequent year. Sharan managed him for 3 weeks and, for some reason, he assigned him to me and said this was to 'test' my management skills.

"Look, I am a little emotional sort of person, but I am very hardworking and I am excellent in whatever I do," he told me while joining my team. Maybe that part is true. I have seen him crying and he was doing that excellently well without any inhibitions.

"You should assign me at least 10 hours of work every day. Without that, I will feel bored," he told me. "Coding is my hobby since school days and software program design is my passion."

"Oh, that is great." I was excited. Those would be the most beautiful words a reportee in IT firm can tell his boss. I am the luckiest boss in this company to have such a great guy in my team. I cursed the manager who had given him below average ratings last year.

Ramu was a short, fat guy. Soon after he joined my team, I realized that his favourite pastime was not coding, but eating snacks which his mother would pack for him every day. He used to bring a big *dubba* full of snacks and as soon as the *dubba* gets empty, he leaves for home. I was more irritated that he would never offer me one of those *pakoda*s even when I went to his cubicle for discussions. He was good not only in crying, but also in eating. I realized what he meant when he said he was excellent in whatever he does most. He was excellent in both the above activities.

Forget about the 10 hour work-day he talked about. Most of the time, he would delay even simplest of the work and I would end up doing it by staying late. Sharan would scold me for the inordinate delay and make an entry in his 'Case Diary'.

I did not have any diary to keep track of the misdeeds of Ramu. But almost all of those 'sins' went into Sharan's diary against my name.

I was on leave during a week. Sharan assigned him a piece of work directly on a Monday. Ramu delayed the work until Friday. That was the first time Ramu unleashed his fatal coding skills in Infopro. He submitted his code to the software library at 5:00 PM on Friday and left for home. The entire system crashed by 5:10 PM due to his code. Sharan called Ramu and he got a 'Do not disturb' SMS. I had just landed in town after my leave and I was asked to come to office by 8:00 PM on Friday. I was blamed by Sharan for not having sufficient 'checks and balances' in my team to ensure good quality code were being submitted. I worked on the Saturday and Sunday. I made numerous phone calls to knowledgeable colleagues to figure out a resolution. By Sunday 8:00 PM, I was able to submit a fix. During the weekend, I got numerous number of 'Do Not Disturb' automated SMSs from Ramu as I tried to reach him on his mobile.

Ramu came in at 11:30 AM on Monday. He directly came to my cubicle.

"You know what—I submitted 100 lines of highly optimized code on Friday," he said proudly.

"Yeah… I know. In fact the entire company knows about it now," I said. "I had to work during the weekend to fix it."

"What?" he couldn't believe it. "Must be because of the old hardware these guys use, which can't execute high efficiency, optimized code. Customer should change the hardware. I can go onsite to work with the customer on that," Ramu kindly offered his service.

"No—no need." I could not control my raised voice.

"Why?" he looked confused.

I calmed down, thought for a moment, and took a deep breath. "No—you have a lot of work to do here—so I won't be able to send you onsite for this." He was not happy about that, but felt good to hear that I thought he had a lot of work at offshore.

My Manager had updated his diary notes on Friday evening itself to add to the list of my misdeeds. He attributed the entire issue to my callousness towards developing my team and not putting stringent quality processes.

I had lost my weekend; got a scolding from my manager and the list of my sins had just grown longer. I looked at Ramu's cubicle. He was enjoying some crispy *pakodas* from his snacks box and listening to some latest Bollywood number on his headphone. He was not even planning to check his mail before lunch, to see if there was any work.

I was thinking about all these when I sat down to fill the appraisal rating for Ramu.

In his self-appraisal form he had explained his contributions to the project, to the company, even to the industry and the larger human race. Anyone who would see that sheet would immediately recommend him for the Nobel Prize, leave alone the system analyst role he was actually targeting in Infopro. He had taken 'responsibility' for the work done by his neighbours and project mates. As the space given to enter self-appraisal description was not enough for him, he added a link to his blog in the appraisal tool mentioning "For more details, please check my blog." I checked the blog and it only had a link to his Facebook account.

I thought of asking Sharan to give me a photo copy of his diary page which listed all my misdeeds so that I could attribute 70% of them to my reportee.

If I gave him the real rating, he would cry like last year and the girls in HR would think that I was a heartless guy. I was not really bothered about other HR folks, but Sayali, the new girl in HR from XLRI, should not think that I am heartless. I may break down if that happens.

I tried to polish my comments as much as possible. But the ratings for most of the tasks had to be 'Needs Improvement' at best. Though I was afraid of the reaction, I could not give any better rating — My work load had increased because of this guy. My sin list in Sharan's Case Diary grew big because of this guy. I had lost many weekends and evenings because of him. And, my appraisal also got screwed up as I had to take 'responsibility' for my appraisee's misdeeds.

I completed his feedback, but did not have the courage to send it to him. I had scheduled his appraisal discussion for the last day of the allowed time.

In the coffee room on Tuesday, Subi had breaking news for me. It seems Ramu was planning to beat up the manager if the ratings were 'unfair' like last time. He feels he should have reacted strongly last time rather than crying. He was determined to correct it this time. His appraisal had to happen in the next 3 days and I panicked big time. I sensed that the situation was graver than I had anticipated.

I asked Sharan if he could handle the appraisal discussion as I would be busy preparing for the project review by quality team on Friday. He refused outright "Boss… handling an appraisal is very easy for me... I don't even need to look at the feedback in advance. I have done hundreds of appraisals. But I want you to do this. I want you to learn."

As the time was running out, I felt weak in my knees. I even thought of resigning just before the discussion. Ramu is at least twice the size as me. Looks like the *pakodas* contain some 'fat creation chemical' as he was becoming bigger by the day. I did not want to have a broken spine for being an upright 'appraisal officer'. I can get a job in another firm, but spine — well, I think it is too costly to get one made of even rubber.

I thought through the night what to do. I could not sleep well.

Next day I saw Ramu at the coffee room.

"Hey, why is Sharan so angry with you?" I asked.

"Is he angry? Why? I don't know?" Ramu was ignorant.

"I had to take his inputs for your appraisal. But he has given me very nasty inputs. It has pulled down your overall ratings. But you don't worry — I will try to give the best I can," I told.

"Shit..." Ramu threw a 300 kg punch on the wall. The wall shook. A portion of the plastering fell down. Some coffee mugs fell down from the table and broke. The people who were having their project meeting in the adjacent conference room ran out shouting 'earth quake'.

"Ramu, I will be busy on Friday with audit prep work. If I am not there, get the feedback discussion done by Sharan. Anyway, it is mainly his inputs which are incorporated in your appraisal feedback."

I looked at Ramu's face. It was red and even some smoke was coming out of his ears and nose. I was afraid his fist would advance towards my chin next. I took 3 steps back. Then started walking slowly and then almost ran to my cubicle.

Discussion was on Friday — which is the last date. On Thursday evening, I reviewed all the task rating and revised them down to 'Unsatisfactory'. In the general comments, I wrote:

"Ramu does not know the basics of coding and commitment is near to zero. His manager ends up doing all his work. Ramu needs to improve himself or should be removed from the team."

After some thought, I added one more sentence. "He should stop eating *pakoda*s in the cubicle or at least offer some to his colleagues."

I submitted the appraisal to Ramu, 15 minutes after he left from office. I know he will check his mails only next day.

Next day morning I sent an SMS to Sharan. "Sir, down with flu. Please take care of Ramu's appraisal."

By afternoon, HR people started questioning Sharan about non completion of appraisal discussion in his team. "This is the last day," Chinthu told him. "If you don't complete appraisal discussion on time, you won't be considered for salary hikes." That threat worked. In fact, such a threat will work anywhere in the IT world!

So finally at 4:00 PM, Sharan called Ramu for feedback discussion.

At home, I spent my time watching the highlights of India–Australia test match. Virender Sehwag was belting the bowlers mercilessly.

That day turned out to be an eventful day at office.

When the famous marathon cry of Ramu had happened, Sharan was at onsite. So, he didn't have any clue about what kind of a person he was going to appraise.

Indeed Ramu had changed his response strategy this time. The rumour I heard was true. As soon as Sharan started reading out the feedback I had written, Ramu interrupted.

"Boss—I have been doing excellent work during the last 1 year. You have given bull shit comments in my appraisal. You know—I was the second rank holder in St. Mary's Convent School in 2002." Ramu raised his voice.

Sharan did not like it. None of his subordinates had ever questioned him back so fiercely.

"Hell with your second rank—as per this feedback, you have done a bull shit job and you deserve a bull shit appraisal feedback." Sharan too was furious.

Ramu couldn't stand Sharan's demeaning of his second rank in St. Mary's. That was his life's biggest achievement till then. And now this bastard PM is belittling it.

Ramu's eyes became bloodshot and face red. He looked like an angry 'Gian' from the cartoon Doraemon. Ramu threw the feedback printout at Sharan's face. Sharan ignored it as it was only a paper. But when it hit his forehead, he realized that there was something inside the paper. It was an old Nokia mobile phone. Just 1 kg weight. As he was inspecting the damages to his forehead, Ramu pushed him. Sharan tripped on a chair and fell on the floor and Ramu tested his nails' sharpness on Sharan's face. It seems Ramu had practiced kick boxing in St. Mary's. He had not mentioned it to anybody only because he had not got any rank in kick boxing. But now he got an opportunity to practice it. First kick was directed at Sharan's stomach and second on his back — a true balancing act. Third one Sharan does not remember, but fourth one was on his bum.

At that time, on my TV, Virender Sehwag was mercilessly beating the pulp out of the Australian bowlers.

After thrashing the PM, as Ramu started to leave the room, Sharan slowly got up from the floor. But soon Sharan realized that it would have been better to lie down and take rest for some more time. When Ramu saw him getting up, he came back to the room again. Failing to control his anger, he pushed Sharan to the floor again and started throwing the marker pens and board erasers at Sharan's face. He tried to literally turn the table on Sharan but the table was too heavy. As he lifted one of the chairs above his head, to throw at Sharan, the facilities manager came running. He was more worried about the chair being damaged. Ramu stormed out of the room. Sharan took rest for some more time on the floor. He is good at learning from mistakes — you know. When he was sure that Ramu was not near the room, he ran out of the room as fast as he could. He suspected that Ramu may return with a gun or a heavier chair.

20 minutes later, instead of Ramu, Sharan was sitting in the HR cubicle, crying aloud. Sharan's reportees watched him from a distance with joy. For them, it was a dream moment to see that their manager was beaten up and he was now crying. Tears were flowing like Niagara fall. Team members rejoiced. They even planned a party at Booze Paradise that evening.

The wounds and bruises on his face were covered with plaster. Since the plaster in our wing's First Aid Box was not sufficient, HR girl got some more from wing B and C.

As Sharan sat there crying, the HR manager was busy searching for the right policy document to be invoked against the culprit.

He was overjoyed when he found one. Ramu was let off last year due to a loophole in policy. But this time, there was no escape.

Ramaswamy was fired on Monday morning. I visited Subi's PG on Saturday and had got some clues regarding the happenings at office on Friday. I decided to take sick leave on Monday too.

Ramu left office with all his belongings at 12:00 noon. After Subi informed me that Ramu had left, I cancelled my sick leave in the second half and joined work at 2:00 PM. When I went to pay my condolences to Sharan, I could not clearly figure out the feelings on his face, as most parts were covered by plaster. But from the wild noises which emanated from inside the plasters covering his face, I guessed he was angry with me.

By the following week, Ramu had printed his visiting card as 'CEO—Thangaswamy Consulting Services and Computer Technology Solutions (TCS-CTS)'. (Thangaswamy was his late father). He declared Steve Jobs as his strength and leading light. He had lined up an interview with *TOI* for next week through one of the friends of his dad.

When I reached office on Tuesday, Subi had put the *TOI* paper at my desk from which Ramu's face was smiling.

In his interview, Ramu lamented that many genius people like him were suffering at the hands of the incompetent managers in big corporates. According to him, there were some managers who would fill bull shit feedback and run away on the day of discussion as they couldn't face the reportee (I took the pen and cut out that sentence on the paper). He exhorted all those suffering geniuses of the corporates to unite. They had nothing to lose but chains created by the incompetent managers. They had a world of opportunities outside.

Sharan found it difficult to face his colleagues and subordinates after the appraisal fiasco. He took transfer to Hyderabad and left a week later. Until he left, he had not removed the plasters from his face so that he could hide his face from everyone.

We presented a goodbye card to him with messages from all of us. One of the messages said:

"My Appraisee has done a great job, else I would have done it myself as you suggested in my appraisal. You had asked me to take responsibility for what my reportee does—but sorry. I won't. I am giving full credit to him for what he achieved. And, by the way, I now understand that project manager also can cry. I saw a photo the other day. Good Luck!"

As Sharan left a PM's post vacant, I am eagerly waiting for the next promotion cycle.

8: The CMM Level 5 Canteen

The Scottish breweries are famous for the century plus old wines they sell. The older the wine is, the costlier the bottle. Rich and famous people queue up to pay millions if it is too old.

Yet, when Infopro canteen served the vegetable soup which was just a week old, that too at a discounted price, it created a ruckus.

On that fateful day, Madhu and team were having a team lunch in the cafeteria. Vanaja had just got married and as a treat for everyone, she ordered veg soup for the entire team.

It was Vanaja who vomited first after drinking the veg soup. Madhu, the PM, extended his hand to congratulate her. He thought it was a pregnancy related sickness. As everyone surrounded Vanaja to congratulate her, on the other side of the table, Vijesh too puked. He too had married recently. People were utterly confused. They knew that anything can happen in Bollywood and Infopro campus, but they did not expect Vijesh to have the pregnancy sickness.

Once Vanaja was taken to the washroom, Madhu turned back to his plate thinking he will continue with his lunch, then he saw a new dish on the centre of the plate on top of his biryani. He was about to try the new dish when Subi stopped him. Subi had just puked into Madhu's plate, when the commotion was going on.

The sound and smell of the pukes echoed from every corner of the dining hall. Since the veg soup was being sold at a discount, the per capita consumption was more that day!

Vanaja was very tired. Madhu dialled the Infopro ambulance. Since ambulance was idle most of the time, the management had decided to rent it to the nearby private hospital as 'Mortuary Van'. That was an additional income for Infopro in these trying times. It showed up as 'Other Income' in the annual report. When Madhu called, Manja, the ambulance driver was on his way to Hosur Public Crematorium, with a dead body. Since Madhu said it was serious, he turned the ambulance and came back to pick up Vanaja. Inside the van, Vanaja and the dead body lied on 2 sides. When they reached the Narayana Hospital, the attendants took out both the bodies and to their horror they found that one was already dead!

"Food poisoning, one senior manager dies in Infopro," said the breaking news of *News9*. It took some time for the Infopro PR team to convince the channel that though the dead body had the looks of a senior manager in IT, he was actually a roadside beggar, who had died in a nearby mental asylum.

So the channel changed the breaking news. "Senior Manager in IT ends up in mental asylum due to work pressure and dies as a beggar."

The PR team decided not to pursue the matter further to avoid making it worse.

Enquiry commission was set up to investigate the food poisoning incident and it submitted the report to Infopro management council within a week. Canteen Manager Shanku was the main accused.

Shanku was in that post for 1 year now and he had been implementing many cost saving initiatives of late. Last October, the canteen had hiked the price of meals and tea. Employees protested. The management constituted a committee to look into the matter. The committee members were from the consulting group within Infopro. They advised canteen management to reduce the rate of hike and look for cost saving ways to ensure profitability. The consultants did not make any direct recommendation, but spoke about reusability, innovative products, etc.

Canteen contractor Sahadev asked Manager Shanku to take up cost saving activities through reusability as the first step.

They started re-using the oil used for frying *pooris*. The same oil would be used for making *pooris* for 4 days, then it would be used for frying the chicken for the next 4 days. By that time, the colour of oil changed to deep black and appeared like crude oil. It was Venu, kitchen staff, who discovered that if he mixed this artificial 'crude oil' with petrol in his bike, the mileage actually increased by 10%.

"Only thing is there will be smell of *pooris* and chicken when your bike goes through the road."

He even made a proposal to independently produce and sell this 'artificial crude oil' commercially.

People used to waste a lot of food in the canteen. Shanku came up with a plan for re-using the same. Instead of collecting the waste in waste bins, he kept clean steel vessels. Separate containers were kept for collecting left over *sambar*, rice, etc. After lunch hours, he took these containers to the nearby 5 star hotel so that they could use it for their dinner buffet. The 5-star guys were also looking for cost cutting ways and it suited them well.

As part of process improvement in kitchen, Shanku asked his folks not to waste time and water in washing fish before cooking.

"These fishes have lived all their life in water only. Why waste time to wash them again?" he would ask.

Sahadev had even congratulated Shanku multiple times for the cost savings he had achieved through the reusability initiative.

However, eventually, it was the same reusability initiative which led him to the veg soup disaster. When there was too much soup leftover on a Friday, Shanku decided to preserve the same until next Friday, when the same soup was part of the menu.

Thus, on that fateful day, many people ended up in hospital. People who did not partake of veg soup that day also took sick leave for the next 5 days so that they didn't have to work. There was no way to check who had taken or not taken the soup.

Sahadev washed his hands off the whole episode and all the blame fell on Shanku.

Next day, before lunch time, Shanku was fired. He tried to present his case based on all the benefits and cost savings he had achieved for the canteen, but no one listened.

Shanku was asked to vacate the premises immediately. He went to his room near the kitchen and packed his bags. Before he left, he took the Vim powder bottle and poured the full bottle into the big *sambar* vessel and left.

As Shanku walked towards the main gate, people were arriving for lunch.

That day was even more eventful than the 'puke day'.

Midway through the lunch, people started running towards the toilets. The 5 toilets in the cafeteria were full in no time. Then people started running towards the toilets in the nearby buildings. In 15 minutes, all the toilets in the campus were occupied. Queues formed in front of toilets. People who came out of the toilet, joined at the end of the queue for the next 'release'.

There was a shortage of water supply that day. So, people got stuck in the toilets as the pipes ran dry soon. Those who were wearing ties could find an alternative for toilet paper. Others stayed back in the toilets.

Dear readers, I know some of you must be questioning your present companies about why you need to wear a tie. You must pick up a lesson or two from this story.

All of a sudden, the campus fell into a deep crisis. Someone called the Disaster Recovery prime to invoke the Business Continuity Plan. But he was also stuck in a toilet and was thinking of ways to escape the disaster he himself was in.

There were long queues in front of the toilets just like people waiting for visa appointments at the Chennai US consulate. As the queue was not moving, people decided to use other alternative places as toilets.

Unable to contain the tsunami brewing in his stomach, Raju went into the old machine design lab. After the GM project closed 2 years back, this lab was not being used anyway. So, using a corner for an urgent requirement is ok, he thought. After all, the biological needs take precedence over any other needs listed in Abraham Maslow's need hierarchy. So, he did not find anything wrong with that.

As he found a dark corner, to his horror, he found that his manager had already occupied that corner. He ran to the other corner and his GM had taken that slot. The GM shouted at him to use the lab booking tool and not to disturb the others. Raju was one of the guys who used to say lab booking tool is an overhead, but now he understood when it is actually required. Without wasting a second, he ran out and disappeared in the garden behind the lab building.

By 3:00 PM, the people in our neighbouring campus, our competitor BTS, complained of strange foul smell from the

Infopro side and those idiots called the fire force saying there was gas leak somewhere.

The fire force arrived with all modern equipment.

The next day's newspapers ran an 8 column story in the front page about all the 'leakages' the fire force found in Infopro.

Infopro got maximum press coverage during that whole week.

Management was furious.

The canteen was closed for 2 weeks for cleaning and renovation.

Employees started going to nearby roadside shops and Darshinis for lunch. They liked the food there even better than the Infopro canteen.

"*Yaar*, we missed this all these times." They lamented.

Canteen opened after 2 weeks. The contractor was removed. The Infopro management decided to run the canteen directly for some time. Facility head was in charge. They asked Rajsekhar from the consulting group to be the operational manager for the canteen until they find a suitable person from outside. Raj had just got transferred from the Mumbai branch. So very few in Bangalore knew him.

Raj protested. "Pradeep Sir, I am a Business Consultant, I can't do this."

"Boss… A business consultant should be ready to work in any business. What is wrong with food and beverages business? Many great management experts work for hotel chains and catering corporations."

"But this is just a canteen."

"Boss, you know you did not do well last year and you are a PIP (Personality Improvement Plan) candidate. You have to take up this assignment and do well. Else you can look for a job outside."

That threat worked and Raj was the Canteen Manager from next day.

After he took over, he started realizing the many challenges in the canteen. Attrition was the main issue.

First day itself, Sanjay, the 'egg counter' man disappeared. So, Raj asked Basavappa, the vessel cleaning guy, to take charge of that counter. He also arranged a 5 minute training session for him on how to make omelettes and bulls-eyes.

First customer at egg counter came at 12:00 noon. Basu poured the broken egg on the pan and then searched for salt. Due to his inexperience, he mistook the fine sugar for salt. After tasting the bulls-eye, customer came back saying that it does not have salt and it seems it is slightly sweet as well. Basu thought maybe he did not add enough salt.

"No problem Sir. I will make you another one. The quality of salt is pathetic these days you know."

Next time again, he took the same *dubba* and put 3 full tea spoons of sugar, thinking it is salt. Customer went to his table with the dish and came back within 30 seconds.

"Boss, this is not Bulls-Eye. This is Bull Shit. This egg is sweet like honey. I lost my money."

Basu was amused at the rhyming words.

"Maybe the hen was diabetic, Sir," Basu was still grappling with what went wrong. But this further infuriated the customer. In a fit of anger, the customer threw the plate at Basu. The plate hit his forehead and Bulls-eye hit his eyes. For that entire week, the egg counter remained closed. Basavappa took sick leave. Raj had to clean the vessels himself in the kitchen. He cursed his fate.

As he was washing the plates, water in the pipe dried up. He asked Chinna to call the plumber.

"Sir, *plumber vlumber kuch naheen kar sakta* sir. Today morning, RK sir was telling his boss on phone that many deals are stuck in the pipeline. Maybe that is the reason sir. RK sir *se baat karo* sir. Maybe he can remove the block."

Raj had to call the plumber himself.

The next day, there was shortage of serving staff at the Meals counter. So, Raj took charge of serving the biryani.

There was a small golf course in front of the canteen. During lunch time, some freshers used to play golf, just to impress the girls having lunch in the cafeteria. Samar was one of them. He was taking a shot at the far end hole, and the ball flew its way into the biryani vessel which Raj was serving. The golfers could not figure out where it had disappeared. They went on searching.

When Raj served one bowl of biryani to GM Rehman, the ball was on top of the rice. Rehman was surprised for a moment. Both he and Raj were not familiar with golf game and its ball.

"What is this new topping? Looks like some gourmet egg," Rehman asked.

Raj had no clue. He remembered the kitchen guy telling yesterday that he was planning to buy Emu egg, which is rarely available but has medicinal values.

"Sir this is Emu egg Sir. Very good for the teeth enamel." Raj put on his quick thinking cap. Rehman did not look convinced. So just like any sales guy, Raj went on to the next selling point "And it also helps growth of hair Sir." His eyes were on Rehman's bald head. That point worked. Like any other bald man, Rehman also fell for it.

"Is It?" Rehman was happy. He had a shaky teeth ever since he had a violent encounter with an auto wallah in Madiwala 3 months back. He thought maybe the Emu egg will fix the teeth problem as well as the hair problem. Two birds with one shot.

"Sir, there is only one emu egg. You are lucky to get it Sir."

Rehman appeared very happy. Today is lucky for me. "Do I need to pay extra?"

"Just 100 Rs Sir." Raj did not know how those words came to his mouth.

Rehman paid 100 Rs to Raj. He was happy that the 2-in-1 medicine was so cheap.

When Rehman sat down at a lone table and started eating his biryani, 2 youngsters came to his table. It was Samar and his friend, who finally found their ball. They were wondering why this guy had kept the ball in his lunch plate.

"Sir, can I take this Sir...?" Samar brought his hand near the ball in Rehman's plate and asked him.

Rehman was flabbergasted. I have paid 100 Rs extra for this Emu egg and these senseless youngsters want to eat it. Don't they have shame? He beat Samar's hands as if chasing a cat which tries to steal the fish from his plate. "Boss I want to eat it. Go buy a meal yourself if you are hungry."

Samar and his friend were stunned. He had heard from Rehman's team members that he eats their head for any work to be done. But he never expected him to eat a golf ball. They walked away confused.

When Raj went inside the kitchen to fill the vessel and came back, he saw there was a small mob around a table. Then he saw someone was being carried by people. He could not see the face. When the 'convoy' reached near the counter, he heard what the patient was talking.

"It was Emu egg … very hard shell… My 2 teeth gone."

The canteen revenue was still way below expectations. It had lost most of the customers to the out-campus Darshinis during the 2-week closure. Most customers never came back.

Even the old manager Shanku had started a small hotel outside Infopro gate and it was getting a lot of customers now.

The Facilities department started questioning the consulting group and their ability to turn around business with their strategies.

Pradeep blasted Raj for not using the right strategies for a turn around. Raj was also clueless. He went through some of his MBA text books to see if there was anything he could adopt. He even sent a mail to his professor in B-School. Professor sent him a list of papers he had published since 1985 and told him he had mentioned the word canteen in one of those articles.

Facilities department reviewed the performance of the canteen and the feedback was 'Unsatisfactory'. Before consulting team took over, the daily sales were 2 lakhs, now it is just 50 thousand Rupees. Pradeep asked Raj to take bold actions or lose his job.

That is when Raj started the '6 pack counter'. In that counter they started serving 'heath food menu' which will help people wanting to achieve 6 pack abs. Price was 100 Rs. Raj himself stood at the counter.

"How many months it will take?" One customer in his late 40s asked Raj while taking his meals from the counter.

"For what?"

"For 6 pack."

"Sir that depends on how many packs you already have." Raj then looked at the questioner. He had a huge tummy. So, this is a 'single sack' guy. This may take 8-10 years even if he eats only this 6-pack meal once a day. An easier way will be to take a sword and cut that tummy into shape. But the hope had to be kept alive so that he would become a 'repeat customer'. "Sir, for you, it may take just above 6 months Sir."

The single sack guy appeared very happy. "Ok Good. So I have to eat this 6-pack meal before lunch or after lunch?"

Raj's mouth opened wide enough to gulp down the guy's huge single-sack. Since people were pushing from behind, the single-sack guy went away thinking he would ask the question the next day.

"Give me a half-meal. I am targeting only 4 packs. I will pay 50 Rs." That was the next guy.

"Sir we are starting separate counters for 4 pack and 5 pack from next week. Here you have to pay full 100 Rs Sir."

All in all, 6-pack counter was a hit. It increased the daily sales by 10K. But still too far from the target.

Sandeep from quality team came to Raj one day. There was team downsizing in quality team, so he wanted to know if Raj could find openings for a couple of quality guys in the 'canteen department'.

"Possible. But they can start only with dishwashing. That is where freshers get posting first. They can move to serving after they get some experience."

"No boss. I am talking about a quality team for the canteen, not for washing," Sandeep explained. "Since the quality of food here is the worst, I believe some of our quality guys can work with you to improve the food quality."

Raj was irritated that Sandeep questioned his food quality. "*Arrey* Boss — you may be able to do something about software quality, but food quality is very tough ... your guys can't do anything."

"Boss... they were part of the team which achieved CMM level 5 for Infopro. They are experts. They can improve quality of anything."

So 2 quality folks, Jomin and Jeevan, got appointed in the canteen. Both guys were fat and looked like Sumo wrestlers.

They would come in the morning and sit in one corner of the kitchen. As soon as some dish becomes ready, they would start eating that.

"What is happening here?" Raj asked one day.

"We're testing the quality of food items," Sumo wrestlers said in chorus.

"Why do you need a full plate of chicken for testing?"

"Boss, we need to do a 'holistic' quality check. Sampling won't work."

"But then, who will pay for the chicken you are eating?"

"Boss — this is called cost of quality — haven't you heard? The cost of quality has to be absorbed by you. Nobody will pay."

After 1 month, there was no improvement in food quality. The only improvement was in the circumference of the 2 Sumo wrestlers.

One day when Raj went into the kitchen, the Sumo wrestlers were measuring the diameter of the hole in *vada*. They were measuring hole sizes for every *vada* and then either eating them or moving it to another vessel.

"What is this? Customers are waiting outside for breakfast. Why are you measuring the holes of the *vada*?"

"Boss, we told you—we are following a 'holistic' approach to quality," Sumo Wrestler 1 appeared angry.

"Ok leave out the hole, and check the quality of the other parts. No?"

"Boss, you know what—our General Motors project got closed because they said there were too many holes in our code. The quality analyst lost his job because of that accusation."

"But that is different. In software you should not have any holes. But for *vada*, hole is a part of it."

"Tell me, why do you need a hole in the *vada*? Can someone eat the hole?"

Raj got confused big time. He never thought about it. As far as he knew, his mother, grandmother and even great grandmother made *vadas* which had holes.

That question had great philosophical dimensions. "Can someone eat the hole in a *vada*? If not, why have it." This is a question some saints can only answer. Not poor me. Raj's mind was blank.

Sumo wrestler 1 continued "Boss, these holes take up valuable real estate in the plate of the customer. Even if someone wants to buy 4 *vadas*, he will buy only 3 because there is no space in the plate."

Raj now understood that the hole in *vada* is a big evil. But he was not sure how to handle.

Discussion then went on in another direction.

"But Boss, you are supposed to give some process improvements for improving efficiency of canteen management." Raj tried to steer the discussion in another direction.

"Of course, we know. We are working on a continuous improvement plan for the canteen."

Next day they came and proposed that the canteen should go for CMM level 5 certification.

"What CMM level 5 — that is for the software projects." Raj was not happy.

"Boss — we have customized the standard. It is now Canteen Maturity Model. We will suggest process improvements and if you follow, your quality will be the highest in the world. You know what — until now, no canteens have got CMM level 5 certified."

"Can I increase the price of *dosa* if I achieve CMM level 5?" Raj asked.

"No."

"Can you ensure more customers come to this canteen if we achieve CMM level 5?"

"We can't guarantee."

"Then why will I go for CMM level 5?"

"Boss, Hell with your silly *vada* and *dosa*. CMM is above all these silly *vada*, chutney, *sambar*. Don't you understand?" The Sumo wrestlers were furious at Raj. Till now, no one in the software industry ever dared to question the CMM standard.

"You know what? Our CEO is committed to CMM level 5. We too are. We will not allow anyone to tinker with CMM. We are even ready to die for CMM."

Raj cursed himself for giving entry space for the quality folks. Now these guys will not leave me until death. As he turned back to look at them, they had already gone to the kitchen to test the quality of chicken 65.

Quality folks asked all the dish washers and cooks to prepare documentation for the work they were doing. Only after that, the canteen could go for CMM assessment. When they refused to do documentation, the Sumo wrestlers threatened to go to the CEO directly. So the poor canteen folks had to agree.

Shivu, the toilet cleaning guy was appointed as the DP prime.

The kitchen staff spent most of the time in quality documentation, quality reviews and DP tool updation. While they were busy with 'quality activities', the *sambar* on the stove got burned, chicken got blackened. But the presence of the Sumo wrestlers in the kitchen forced them to stick to their 'quality' related work. They were now afraid of the wrestlers.

Due to the burned *sambar*, overcooked rice 'paste' and blackened chicken, the sales in canteen plummeted further. Kitchen staff had to spend too much time complying with the CMM standards and it left little time for cooking. Hence a lot of food got wasted.

After a hectic Friday, when Raj got out of the office at 8:00 PM, Shanku was waiting for him at the gate.

"Sir, how is it going Sir?"

"Not good Shanku, these days, all employees are going outside for lunch."

"Sir if you don't mind, I will tell you something Sir."

"Tell me."

"You know I started this small hotel 3 months back. I am getting a lot of customers, especially from Infopro. I am not able to service the complete demand. I have expanded my place, but my kitchen has limited capacity."

"If you don't mind, I will buy the meals from you Sir. I will sell it in my shop. That will be additional revenue for you so that you can meet your target."

"But what about the burned food — there is a lot of burning these days as kitchen folks are busy complying to the CMM level 5 guidelines."

"No problem sir, we can sell the CMM level 5 food directly to the *gobar* gas plant sir ... good money no, Sir. I know one Thimmaia Gowda who is running the plant. He is badly in need of raw material."

Raj couldn't believe. That is a great idea. So after all, there is some use because of CMM.

He discussed with his manager Pradeep. He agreed, as the overall revenue will now be close to the daily target given by management. "It is just another channel for selling your product. Our aim is to achieve the daily sales target." That was Pradeep's opinion.

After Shanku, other Darshinis also queued up to meet Raj. Someone from Malaysia called the other day. He is running a fertilizer manufacturing plant in Kuala Lumpur. He is willing to import the food from Infopro canteen directly so that it can be used as a raw material for his fertilizer plant. He can give a good price as well.

So finally, with revenues from the Malaysian businessman, Raj was able to meet the daily target set for him by the management.

Raj realized that it was actually the CMM level 5 initiatives which saved the canteen. He went to thank the quality folks.

The Sumo wrestlers were in the kitchen. They were searching for unburned chicken pieces to do some more 'holistic testing'.

With the great turnaround achieved, Raj was out of PIP and was back in a major assignment in an investment bank in Singapore. The Sumo wrestlers were given full responsibility of the canteen operations.

What Raj last heard was that these days no one goes to canteen for lunch or breakfast. There is a direct pipeline from the canteen kitchen to the fertilizer plant set up by the Malaysian tycoon near Electronic City! The canteen is now the most profitable business arm of Infopro, leaving the software verticals far behind.

9: Cultural Program Turns Cultureless Program

Our project was supposed to be completed on October 15th, but instead we were completing it on October 1st.

I know — you must have already started typing a congratulatory mail to us. Hold on! Let me complete.

I didn't tell which year October. The original deadline was last year October 31st, and we are finishing it in this year October!!!

Now, discard that draft congratulatory mail if you would like and read on.

You probably know this—One year delay is no surprise for the Infopro's now famous global project delivery. There were projects which got delayed by 6-8 years. Some of the clients went bankrupt funding our projects year after year. One client CEO had even committed suicide and another CFO had been admitted to mental hospital.

In case of this project we are talking about, the client company was still in business and they were getting some software from us, though 95% scope had to be cut off to meet the revised deadline of Oct 15th of this year.

Group Manager Rehman and Project Manager Madhu agreed to go ahead with team outing, to celebrate the project completion. This was the first project which had delivered something, despite the fact that it was managed by Madhu and Rehman!

Madhu is not only the PM, but also the CEO (Chief Entertainment Officer) of the project. He arranges for project parties, team building events, etc. The spelling and grammar mistakes in his mails are also a free source of entertainment to the team mates.

Once Madhu had to send a mail to the team asking them to come to the 'Edison' training room for the inter-project training course in the account. His mail read as below:

"Hi Team, Please proceed to Room 1 for the project intercourse. Arun and Shwetha will anchor the same today". The room was full and overflowing that day, with even people from other accounts wanting to join!

Next day, he even got calls from competitors asking if he would like to offer the same session for the outside market.

When the project team celebrated its first phase release last year, Madhu had arranged a cultural program by the team members. Sandhya danced to the tune of *Choli ke piche* and the video had gone viral. So much so that Ram Gopal Verma offered her the role of a *bhoot* doing item dance in his next venture 'Ram Gopal Verma Ki Bhoot'. She has applied for a long leave to go for the shoot.

This time too, Madhu wants to celebrate success with a memorable team building plus a wonderful cultural program. He wants everyone in the team to participate in the cultural program.

He wrote a macro in an excel and using that identified a performing item for everyone in the project.

Rehman, Group Manager was Madhu's boss. GM was dreaded by the entire team. He had joined from another company a year back and ruled the project like an autocrat. He would come for code reviews/ document reviews and try to prove that all the code, all the documents were useless. He never gave good appraisal feedback to anyone. He was good in finding the errors and mistakes in everyone's performance. So, people hated him.

Madhu's excel macro had identified 'Bharatanatyam' as the item for Rehman.

Asking him to do Bharatanatyam was like asking an elephant to do a head-stand. The only time he used to dance was after his pub sessions on Saturdays. Dancing after boozing is a separate art form in itself. Though the Government of India has not recognized it as a separate art form, the Bangalore police have done so. Once Rehman was picked up from MG Road for performing this item on the road.

Rehman checked YouTube for some Bharatanatyam performances to see if he could modify his 'bar dance' a little bit to make it 'Bharatanatyam' somehow. But after seeing the BN on YouTube, his confidence subsided. Forget about swaying the neck, he could not even turn his head to look at someone calling from behind. His entire body had to be turned if he wanted to look back. It was like changing the entire software to repair one simple bug. He had a neck collar since last 1 year.

Rehman finally got Debabrata to do a barter. Deba had got group dance. Deba is known as Mandela for the similarity in looks. Be it a group dance or Bharatanatyam, both are same for him. He doesn't know the 'abcd' of both.

With a 4 feet wide body frame, Mandela's other nickname was 'Haathi'! He was our project football team goalkeeper. When he stood in front of the goal posts, it was very difficult for the opposite team players to locate a gap between his body and the goalposts. He never had any stage frights. He didn't mind doing Bharatanatyam or break dance or belly dance as the situation demands.

There was a dance teacher in his neighbourhood in Madiwala and he decided to ask her for help with the choreography.

"I will do the group dance alone," Rehman told Madhu, as no one came forward to dance with him.

Madhu thought for a moment. In last 10 years of his experience as the 'CEO', he had never witnessed anyone performing group dance alone. Can this be used as an opportunity for 'introducing innovation in the project' and claim some bonus points in the appraisal?

"Let's try till tomorrow to get people. I will also try to find. If we don't get, then you can do it alone."

Meanwhile, everyone started their respective rehearsals.

"Rehman..." Madhu called from behind as he was walking towards the cafeteria for lunch. He stopped and turned his entire frame as the neck had become an 'immovable property'. By the time he completed the half rotation, Madhu caught up.

"Man, I have found a few junior folks to dance with you." He started. "I have promised them biryani after the program. You will have to sponsor it. Reshma, Chinku, Patil, Sonu, Prakash — all of them will be there."

"Whatever. Fine with me." Rehman was relieved.

"Sonu suggested you can do Lungi dance. Since you have Shah Rukh's looks, it would be apt."

Shah Rukh's looks…? Rehman wanted to jump with joy — he did not do it only because he feared the neck collar may fall off.

Rehman went to YouTube and watched 'Lungi Dance'. He imagined himself in the place of Shah Rukh and enjoyed the video thoroughly. He even started having a crush on Deepika Padukone!

He took a photo of himself and that of Shah Rukh Khan and projected side by side on his laptop screen and tried to find similarities. The only similarity was that both had 2 eyes and a mouth. Every organ in Rehman's face was specially tweaked for worse before 'deploying' it in his face. It was like the software we just submitted to our customer — Ugly/Unclean with a lot of pitfalls. But Rehman was able to find out some similarities after thorough search and he got excited. It seems his eyebrows and Shah Rukh's eyebrows were of the same colour.

"I need to get some lungis now from the mallu folks in the project." He decided on the action plan for next day morning.

He asked Thomas John to supply him some lungis. He had recently joined the project from Trivandrum CET.

"Lungi…?" Thomas gave a surprise look "I don't have any."

"Maan...! You don't have one…? You are a mallu and you don't have a lungi..." Rehman was shocked. His mouth opened wide enough to swallow a rabbit, as if he just heard an Eskimo telling that he has not seen snow. "Maan...! This is too much... I have heard that even your chief minister goes to office wearing a lungi."

Thomas tried to explain how the middle-class folks in Kerala have upgraded themselves to Bermuda from Lungi. In fact, that was the only progress in Kerala in the last decade.

Rehman checked with HR if there was any Lungi Allowance just like the suit allowance. HR confirmed it was not there. He again sent a follow up question to them asking if the 'LTA' mentioned in the salary component represented Lungi and Tie Allowance or something else. While he waited for an answer, he decided to borrow the lungis from the mallu guys working in the Infopro canteen.

Canteen folks told they could lend the lungis for a fee, but only for the final program and not for rehearsals. They said there was lot of demand for their lungis after the Lungi Dance became a hit. So, next month onwards they would charge higher amount for lungi rentals.

Due to lack of lungis, the artists decided to do rehearsals using bathroom towels. The bathroom towels rehearsal had to be soon stopped because of two reasons. One, the dormitory staff came and complained that the towel numbers were dwindling on a daily basis and two, the bathroom towels were meant to be robed inside the bathroom which is a completely covered place and not on a dance floor in which, with every move the towel falls down. The dance team members started picking the fallen towel so frequently that someone watching thought it was a dance step. Because of these difficulties, it was decided to use imaginary lungis for practice.

Dance practice started that same evening. After 5 minutes into the rehearsal, it was decided that there should not be any dance steps involving neck movements. After 10 minutes, they decided to cut down on 'knee' movements as well—again, for uniformity! After all, GM's decisions were final!

Meanwhile, Mandela was making some progress on the Bharatanatyam front.

He went to the dance class near to his PG.

"You want to get your kid admitted for dance classes?" teacher asked Mandela as she saw him.

"No Ma'am. It is for me… I was a dancer in my school days… I want to 'freshen up' my skills now as I have to take part in a program in my company."

He then spent 5 minutes to convince her that he was still a bachelor and did not have kids. He may look like a 40 year old mature man only because he was taking care of a lot of responsibilities at office, and was on his way to become a mature project manager.

Looking at Mandela's 6 feet tall-4 feet wide enormous frame, she refused initially. Then she remembered her guru's advice—

don't deny teaching any potential student—especially when he/she is ready to pay. So, Mandela became a dance student.

The classes were run on the first floor. On the second day, the ground floor shop owner complained to the teacher that a part of the roof plastering had fallen on his head. He saw Mandela standing by the corner, sweating profusely.

"Your father has also come to visit your classes?" he asked the teacher.

"No it's my student."

"Student?" The shop owner Heeralal could not hold back his shock.

"Aisa shishya hai to, plastering hi naheen ... poora building neeche aa jayega ... aap ki classes ke liye koyee doosra building dhoondo..."

He looked at Mandela again and walked away.

After 5 minutes, the lady staying on the 2nd floor came down. It seems the *sambar* vessel she had kept on the stove fell down because of the frequent shakes to the building. She had done some initial investigation and found that the epicentre of the quake was in the dance class.

The teacher called Mandela to a corner and congratulated him for 'quickly picking up' the lessons she had taught. She then explained why he may not need to attend classes regularly. Since he was very talented, he could learn from YouTube directly. If he had any doubts, he could send a SMS to the teacher and she would send a prompt response. Teacher was active even on 'WhatsApp' as well. She could even refund the fees he had already paid.

Mandela was disappointed that he couldn't now practice alongside the college girls who were in the class, but the prospect of saving a few 1000 rupees motivated him to consider the proposal given by the teacher.

Meanwhile Amit Vaswani was preparing for the skit.

Amit is the Business Analyst in our project. Though his title is 'BA', he is one guy who tries to analyze anything under the sun. Since there was no role called 'Universal Analyst', he settled for a mere 'Business Analyst' role in Infopro.

Amit had already started working on his drama script for the cultural eve. It was a crime thriller where a murder happens in an IT firm and a BA takes up the investigator's role. He solves the mystery in 5 days. He progresses gradually through his investigation in the first 4 days. On the 4th day evening, he has almost narrowed down on the culprit, but he gets attacked by some goons when he walks towards home from the bus stop at night in Koramangala. However, he escapes unscathed, as he is a Karate black belt. A special project meeting is called on 5th day. The BA explains what all leads he had got in the past week, what all inferences he made and how he identified the real culprit. The culprit was none other than the Project Manager.

He narrated the story to Madhu and Veena — the PM and TL.

Madhu did not like the fact the BA is made the hero. More than that, he got irritated that the PM is made the villain.

"*Abey*… why is the project manager made the villain…? And BA the hero?" He could not control his anger. "*Chalo*... make the PM the hero and you can have the GM as the villain." He suggested.

"But our story demands…" Amit tried to convince.

"Nothing doing… Don't tell me these kind of excuses which an actress gives after doing a 2 piece scene in the pool."

"But if the PM is the villain, it will look very natural to the audience." Amit's reasoning further infuriated Madhu.

Finally as a compromise formula, they decided to ditch that story and go for a new one, which mixes a modern story with a traditional setting. Amit decided to base it on the Ramayana—an age old theme used multiple times in the campuses across India.

Amit came up with a storyline which superposed an IT industry rivalry into the Ramayana storyline.

Lanka Software and Kishkindha Software are competitors. Kishkindha Software is founded by 3 HR professionals—Bali, Sugreeva and Hanuman. Lanka Software is run by a 6.5 feet tall dark money lender called Ravan. Surveillance and Information Technology for Aviation (SITA) is the latest software product developed by Kishkindha Software. Ravan steals the same and wants to re-label it as 'Made by Lanka Software'. Ramankutty, the architect of the software, is out to save SITA from Ravan. Kishkindha bosses Sugreeva and Hanuman support him to the hilt using their money, contacts, workforce and even a B1 Visa to Lanka.

HR team heard about the story and they vehemently objected, for some unknown reason.

So, finally Amit decided the tried and tested formula—go with the original Ramayana.

Story decided, they needed to now move on to the next step—Casting. They sat on the couch in the lobby and started casting—the exercise was led by Amit (director cum script writer), Madhu (Project Manager and one of the main actors) and Subi (Software Engineer cum Amit's assistant director).

There was no doubt on who would become Sita. Project beauty Suma was unanimously chosen. Ravan's role was auctioned at first. In the selected script, Ravan had more close scenes with Sita; so, there was big fight for who would do Ravan's role.

Srinivas, the thinnest fellow in the project wanted to do that role. He even started dreaming about Sita abducting scene rehearsals. But Amit cut it out saying Srinivas can be only used in the scene where the solider stands with a spear. He offered the role of either the soldier or the spear. Srini refused both.

Finally, Mandela was chosen as Ravan. Hearing the decision, Suma told she could not do Sita's role. She even proposed that her BF, who was in a different project and a regular gymmer, could do the role of Ravan instead. However, Mandela pointed to the rule book saying that only this project people could perform.

Later that day, Mandela gave a treat to his friends for bagging the role of Ravan.

Next was Rama's role auction. Madhu wanted to play the role of Rama. He thought that it would further boost his image and improve his visibility and he would get the best shot at next year's GM promotion. Madhu thought Amit would easily accept his suggestion as he was his PM, after all.

But director had other ideas — what he offered to Madhu was the role of Sugreeva.

Madhu got infuriated again— "Boss, for the role of Sugreeva, you will get many people. Our DM Rehman will be very natural fit for 'Sugreeva'. No makeup required on face. He just needs a tail. Let's decide on Rama's role which I can portray well."

"Madhu, Sugreeva's role will be apt for you as audience will be able to better relate." Amit tried to convince.

"Boss—what are you saying…?" That was beyond tolerable limits for Madhu.

"I mean, Sugreeva is very strong and assertive. Just like you." That calmed Madhu a bit.

"Rama is soft, brave, young, tall and handsome. I am yet to decide on whom to give Rama's role. We need a good actor with good physique."

"Boss… Have you seen Rajini sir … and what all roles he plays?" Madhu was not ready to leave it "In my primary school, I had got the best actor award for my role as Rama."

Arguments continued. It was going out of control. Subi had to stop the 2 thespians from getting physical. More people joined the couch where casting was happening.

"I can give my script only if I get Rama's role," Amit shouted.

"Your script … huh…? Boss… Valmiki Gupta has written the Ramayana. You are just doing a copy paste."

People around were surprised to hear the surname of Valmiki.

"Valmiki Gupta…?" Subi looked at Madhu with a question mark on his face.

"Sorry… Valmiki Sharma…" Madhu wanted to close that discussion. It did not matter if Valmiki was a Gupta or Sharma. The fact is that he wrote the Ramayana, not Amit Vaswani, this useless BA in Infopro.

"See… My script is not exactly Ramayana as written by Valmiki. I have included my views and interpretations of the epic in my script," Amit explained.

"I know… You want to be the hero… So you want me to take up some unimportant role." Madhu then thought for a moment and came down a bit "*Chalo*… then let me take up Lakshmana's role."

But Amit had some reservations "See, Lakshmana is Rama's younger brother. If you play Lakshmana and I play Rama, people will think why the younger brother looks 10 years older than the elder one. Lakshmana will look like the father of Rama."

Again, arguments and counter arguments. Subi kept the 2 from firing the first punch.

DM Rehman came running on hearing the commotion. So, people left the decision to the 'high command'.

Amit provided an executive summary of the problem at hand. "See, we are deciding on the actors for each role in this Ramayana skit. We have decided to give you a double role." Rehman felt very happy and thankful to Amit. From his LKG days, no one had offered him any role in the skits — forget about the double role he just bagged. So, now, as a display of gratitude, he was ready to support anything which comes from Amit.

"I want Madhu to play the role of Sugreeva. It is a very complex role which can be effectively portrayed by an actor of a high calibre. And the fact that the image of Madhu matches that of Sugreeva."

"True, I agree…" Rehman nodded, though he could not connect Sugreeva and Madhu. He thought it was about the looks.

"If the matching of image is the criteria, then you should play the role of 'Shakuni'." Madhu shouted at Amit.

But the 'high command' decisions were favourable to Amit, the director.

Finally as the casting came to an end and people dispersed, Rehman was too eager to know about his double roles "So, which are the 2 roles I have to play? Is it Rama and Lakshmana?" He asked trying to hide the excitement.

"Jambawan and Bali," Amit told casually.

Rehman was speechless. He couldn't imagine Shah Rukh Khan playing the role of Jambawan. But now there was no other way but to accept. "Shit…! I should have asked this in the beginning." Given a choice, he wanted to cancel all the decisions he made about the casting and give the role of Rama to Madhu.

He quickly remembered that though the name of Shakuni came up, no one was assigned that role. He thought of a last attempt.

"Amit, Since Jambawan is an old chap, maybe you can give that to someone else. Instead, can I play the role of Shakuni?"

"Shakuni…? In Ramayana…?" Rehman did not understand why Amit was so surprised at his question.

"Sir, we need someone strong for Jambawan's role. He looks like a monkey, but he is a saint. He is wise and even advices Hanuman!"

Rehman heaved a sigh of relief. So Jambu is a saint, not a monkey. Thank God.

Final program day.

During the daytime, HR took the team through some team building games at the resort. After evening snacks, all dancers, actors and singers went to the green rooms for the makeup. The HR team, our VP, the resort employees also were part of the audience. We had invited our neighbouring project members also for the event. DM Rehman and PM Madhu had even invited their families.

Skit was the most awaited program as Amit had given a lot of mouth publicity.

Mandela's Bharatanatyam ended when a UFO (Unidentified Flying Object) hit his head. The object was later identified as a *chappal.*

The skit started from the scene where Maareecha took the form of a deer and appeared before Sita. Upon Sita's insistence, Rama decides to chase the deer. As per script, Rama chased the Rakshasa and went out of the stage. Immediately thereafter, there was a cry for help from Rama. He had actually fallen off the edge of the stage. People thought the cry was part of the skit. Later Lakshmana draws the Lakshmana Rekha and leaves. He had taken a marker from conference room to draw the Lakshmana Rekha — but as usual the marker was not working. So, LR remained an imaginative circle, just like the equator. Ravan comes as a *bhikhari* and kidnaps Sita. Mandela came in as Ravan.

Even after Lakshmana came back to the ashram, there was no trace of Rama. For a moment Lakshmana thought that maybe both Rama and Sita were kidnapped by Ravan. Sugreeva and Hanuman had completed makeup and were having a smoke at the back of the stage. When they heard about the mysterious disappearance of Rama, they started searching for him. They finally found him by the side of back stage struggling to get up on his feet. His leg had got stuck between 2 wooden pieces which supported the stage. Sugreeva and Hanuman lifted Rama on their shoulders and put him back on stage, near Lakshmana. Sugreeva still had a burning cigarette in his mouth.

Audience tried to remember if such an incident was part of the original Ramayana where a smoking Sugreeva and Hanuman carry Rama back to his ashram after killing of Maareecha.

Rama was groaning in pain but somehow finished his dialogues.

Next scene was in Lanka. Ravan, with his 10 heads, is having a conversation with Sita and he laughs like Amrish Puri. Ravan completed that scene beautifully, laughed like a real villain throwing his head back. But that action was detrimental. Ravan's crown, to which 9 other heads were attached, lost its grip and fell on Sita's lap. Ravan stood there with only one head — the ugliest among the 10. Sita was sobbing thinking about Rama and suddenly Ravan's heads were in her lap. She was totally confused about what to do. She wanted Rama to cut off the 10 heads of Ravan, but 90% of them were already in her lap. It was like 90% of the project got completed before kickoff.

Now, it will be a waste of time if Rama travels to onsite — Lanka — for just the last 10%. She thought for a moment and decided to 'act responsibly' as Madhu had asked her in appraisal feedback. She stood up and placed the crown and heads on Ravan's remaining head. Ravan even said 'Thank You'. The audience clapped. For sure, they liked the small twist in the story.

Angada came to Ravan's palace and he was supposed to read out a message from Rama. Sapan, who came as Angada, had not slept the previous night due to a major issue detected in staging server. He had taken a printout of the message 2 days back, so that he could just read it out. Since the role was simple, he did not even do rehearsals and focused on the P1 issues in his module.

Unfortunately, when he came to stage, by mistake he had taken some other paper onto the stage. Still in the sleepy mood, he started reading out from the paper. It was the printout of someone's personal feedback.

"You need to be assertive," Angada told Ravan. Ravan was confused. Even after doing this much, these guys think I am not assertive!

"You have to show innovation and creativity." A bit more confusion. I own the Pushpak (only jumbo jet of the times) and still people doubt my innovation.

"You need to do more of what you were doing and show leadership in every action," Angada continued. Ravan was confused big time. He had kidnapped Sita and Rama wants him to do more of that! "Was she troubling Rama so much...? May be a case of reverse domestic violence..." Ravan was trying to find the reason.

"You can have a big picture, but need to attend to each and every detail." Ravan was embarrassed to the core. This is too much; I am not that kind of person. Ravan felt like running away from Lanka.

Angada had forgotten to leave his mobile behind before entering Ravan's court. It started ringing now. His caller tune was '*Why this Kolaveri Kolaveri Dee...*" So, Ravan's court was now filled with a lot of confusion and a loud *dappamkoothu* song.

For a moment, even Sita thought that it was audio message from Rama for her.

Amit, who was in backstage in the attire of Rama, realized things were getting out of hand. He was the director. He couldn't allow it to continue. So he himself came on stage and stood in front of Ravan. He conveyed the original message. Also added a statement

"The message is so important. That is why I decided to come myself."

People clapped and appreciated the twists and tweaks the director had brought in the story.

Sugreeva's scenes were over; he met Angada on the backstage. They decided to go for a quick smoke. As they were away from stage, Sugreeva told Angada...

"*Saala chootiya woh Jambawan kya acting kar rahaa hai...? Kisne de diya usko role?*" Madhu, who was in Sugreeva's attire, was secretly criticizing his boss Rehman's acting. As he had forgotten to remove the wireless mike from his dress, the criticism got relayed to the entire audience. People thought it may be the invisible '*Kaal Purush*' who was giving a running commentary.

Jambu, who was on stage, giving some advice to Hanuman, was caught unawares. He knew Madhu's voice very well.

"*Saale ko acting ka abcd bhee nahin maloom ... double role karne aaya hai ... sala kutte ka bachcha...*" Madhu continued his review of Rehman's acting. People started listening more to the review than the boring advice Jambu was offering to Hanuman.

Jambu was in 2 minds — to continue advising Hanuman or to ask him to wait for a minute, go to back stage, beat up Sugreeva and come back to stage to continue the advice. Even Hanuman was listening more to the words of Sugreeva now. Jambu decided that it was useless to advise Hanuman. As per script, he would anyway jump to Lanka. So he concluded the advice by asking Hanuman to jump 'ASAP' and rushed to backstage to settle scores with Sugreeva.

When Rama and Ravan had a fierce battle on stage, behind the stage, Sugreeva and Jambu had a fierce verbal duel. Sugreeva tried to use the '*Gada*' in his hand, whereas Jambu was in free hand mode. Angada, Vibheeshana, Indrajith and Kumbhakarna somehow pacified Jambawan and Sugreeva.

Audience thoroughly enjoyed the entire drama. By the time Ravan was beheaded and Rama took re-possession of Sita, some people were rolling on the floor laughing.

Lungi Dance was the climax program.

There was complete chaos in the green room. First, the lungis were small. Second, they were not washed and were smelly. They smelt of chicken, mutton, *sambar*, *rasam* and even the special *Rajastani kheer* served last year. Rehman was still in Jambawan makeup. As he had to spend his time in an unplanned battle with Sugreeva, he did not get time to remove his makeup.

The lungi could hardly cover the circumference of Rehman. When he was literally struggling to 'meet the 2 ends', Manoj suggested to him to remove his pants and wear only the lungi so that it would comfortably fit. That idea worked and Rehman decided on the spot that Manoj should be given 'exceeded expectations' on the innovations front. So, to reduce the circumference, Rehman removed his jeans and wore only lungi. He realized he had not even removed the tail of Jambu. He hid his tail under the lungi.

"Now, our beloved GM Rehman and party will dance to the tune of Lungi Dance." The announcement was received with thunderous applause as the team members were quite eager to watch the GM dance.

When the curtain went up, Sonu's lungi also went up with the curtain, as it got stuck in some pin on the curtain. Luckily his Bermuda saved the moment for him. People were trying to read the writing on his Bermuda— 'Made of Steel'. As people started wondering what is made of steel, he somehow reclaimed the lungi from the curtain and tied it around his waist.

The sight of a bulky, bald guy like Rehman dancing on stage itself was a big entertainment for the audience. When Rehman saw that the people were laughing, he thought they were thoroughly enjoying the show. That gave him huge motivation and excitement. He forgot his knee pain, and started jumping around with all his energy. The belt which kept the lungi on his waist was not tied to withstand the kind of pressure it was subjected to. Finally it gave way the little hold it had on Rehman's waist.

Rehman was now dancing on the stage in a dirty underwear, with a tail on his back and monkey make up on the face. The underwear itself was an antique piece with several holes in it, as if specifically designed for natural ventilation.

"Hey is that tail a real one...?" TL Veena was asking Sumit, who was sitting next. Veena was not very familiar with male anatomy.

Rehman saw that the audience were laughing and enjoying too much. He was happy and proud. Because of the neck collar, he could not see beneath and he did not realize that the lungi was now on the floor, not on his waist. And he was not wearing pants or Bermuda. The group dance had just turned into a cabaret dance. People had already started sharing the video with their friends through WhatsApp.

His co-performers stopped midway and ran away to the back of the stage one by one, as soon as they realized the magnitude of the mishap. Nobody wanted to shout that the King was nude! Sonu came back to the stage only to take a picture of the hero of the day. The resort manager came running and he asked his folks to down the curtain. The resort manager had been arrested a year before for 'running a dance bar in the resort illegally' and he feared he may get arrested for what was going on stage.

After the curtain fell, Rehman realized that the stage was empty. There was one dirty lungi lying on the stage. As he tried to lift the tip of his lungi and fold it, he realized that there was only a VIP Frenchie between him and the outside world! A VIP Frenchie, which had too many holes — some as big as French windows.

Not just the earth, the entire solar system started to revolve around his head. He thought of running away to the Bannerughata forest and staying back there for rest of his life!

In 5 minutes, people saw a Maruti Swift speeding away through the back gate of the resort. It was in a hurry as it hit 2 large plant pots and almost ran over a security guard at the gate.

Rehman couldn't sleep. He did not know how to face his subordinates in office.

Next day, the HR Manager told Madhu and team that Rehman had resigned with immediate effect. He would collect his belongings from office on Saturday evening 10:00 PM, after even the daytime security has left.

After that fateful day, Rehman lost his job, but he got a call from Colors TV for two programs— 'Dancing with the Stars' and 'Big Boss'. It seems, it is a good place to make some money once you lose your job due to unpredictable circumstances. Even some former cricketers have done that.

Rehman shifted his house to Mumbai. He now owns a posh apartment in Mumbai and is signed up for the next Shah Rukh Khan movie for the role of a comedian.

10: Bon Voyage — An Infoproite's adventures at onsite

Its no kidding…

The statisticians across the world are appalled by this phenomenon in Infopro…

A few Amsterdam based data scientists even confirmed that they observed this phenomenon not just in Infopro, but in fact in all the IT firms in India…

Here is the statistical problem. You pick any 2-3 year experienced IT professional in India and ask them what is their wish, 99% of the time, the answer is "I want to go onsite". Rest 1% are busy preparing for CAT exam and they have lost touch with the external world. This 99% probability of a real life situation has turned out to be an enigma and is not yet solved by even the Russian scientists who came up with the famous normal distribution curve. This has not been able to be explained by any distribution curve so far.

As expected, Mohit was also not an outlier and was well within the distribution. He had 3+ year experience and his ambition was also to go onsite. His cousin Dhiraj had joined IT industry 2 years back and he had made 3 trips to onsite already. Dhiraj's mother would ask Mohit's mom every other day when is Mohit going onsite? For Mohit's mom, his onsite had now become '*Izzat ka sawaal*'–a 'matter of honour'. Either Mohit should go onsite in next 3 months or she would have to go to Kashi and spend the rest of her life there. She had already informed Mohit about her decision.

To achieve his onsite goal, Mohit tried all political, spiritual and emotional ways in the past 1.5 years. A part of his Time and Material (Meaning Time and Salary) was dedicated to temples for praying for this. He visited Shiva temple on Monday, Devi temple on Tuesday, Ayyappa temple on Wednesday, Hanuman temple on Thursday and Ganesha temple on Friday. On weekends, he went to two temples.

He went to the ashram in Bangalore outskirts and met Swamiji. He enquired if the Swamiji could be an aggregator between him and the different gods. He was ready to pay all the fees at the ashram. But the Swamiji should directly take up his case with all the gods and get his 'onsite wish' executed on a 'Tatkal' basis. Swamiji kindly accepted the fees and when he asked if the deal was pukka, Swamiji told something in Sanskrit.

That was 2 months back and, for some reason, the Tatkal plan did not work out.

Of late, he had even started visiting churches and mosques. This was because he came to know that his colleagues John and Rasool had started submitting their onsite requests in church and mosque. Now, Mohit not only had to frequently submit and resubmit his own prayers at his favourite temples but also needed to make some counter-prayers at the mosque and church so that John's and Rasool's requests could be slowed down a bit.

Actually, God himself got bored with the repeated requests from him.

Mohit had moved three projects in the last 1.5 years. The pasture seemed greener on the other side always. Whenever he saw an onsite potential and moved to a new project, the onsite would have been already taken by someone. Now, he had run out of all reasons to jump to a new project and his delivery manager had strictly told him to continue in the current project for next 2 years.

From an emotional perspective, he had used all sentimental family stories such as a deep financial crisis in the family, father being bed ridden, sister's marriage held up, etc. His project managers were successfully able to investigate these stories and bust them all. The untold secret in Infopro is that when such emotional requests are raised and contends with another onsite enthusiast, the manager tells the affected person to investigate and confirm if the story is true or taken from a Bollywood movie. Mohit's contenders had so far been successful. His financial crisis story was busted as someone managed to find out that Mohit had booked an expensive bike soon after this story was published for project manager's consumption. After his father's ill fate story was published, someone managed to find a photograph of his family touring in Goa from Facebook. Also, it was proved that Mohit's sister is just a Class 12 student and the family had no plans of marrying her off any time soon. To test this, actually Rasool had sent a letter to Mohit's father saying he would like to marry Mohit's sister without dowry! After these incidents, Mohit was given the warning that one more false excuse he brings, he would be permanently taken out of the onsite list.

Thus, the only thing he can do now is to pray and wait.

In the meantime, his mother confirmed her tickets in the 'Banaras Express' for next month. She was unable to bear Dhiraj's mothers' bragging anymore.

Not sure which of the prayers of Mohit worked, but an unexpected opportunity arose in the project all of a sudden.

Vikram, a long time onsite person in the project, was refusing to return. He initially went for 6 months, but it was already 3 years. He told the customer that he was the most intelligent engineer in Infopro and any replacement he may get at onsite, would turn out to be a disaster. To make his case stronger, Vikram also told the customer that he hailed from a poor family in a Mumbai slum and he needed to be at onsite at least for 5 years to pay back all his loans and to buy a house. He even told that Jamal, Salim and Lata from *Slumdog Millionaire* were his childhood buddies and 'slum mates' in Mumbai. By the time he completed his story, the customer was almost in tears.

The Project Manager Surya tried his level best to break the jinx and bring back Vikram, but, needless to say, he failed miserably.

Now, a short-term additional work had come in the project and Surya wanted to use this as a double opportunity. He called Mohit on a Wednesday morning for a meeting.

Mohit had just arrived that day as he had to go to the Ayyappa temple in Madiwala and then come to office. He was least expecting what was in store for him.

Surya started,

"Mohit, we considered your aspiration to go onsite and we are giving you an opportunity."

Mohit was excited; he never thought he would ever hear these words. He silently offered two three more offerings to the gods.

"Thanks Surya, tell me what I should do…"

Surya looked sternly at Mohit's face "There is some risk and commitment required from you…"

Mohit was now remembering some movie scenes in which the villain tells the hero that you can take the money but only after fulfilling certain conditions.

"See, you know that Vikram has been in onsite for long. We will send you onsite for a small project of 3 months and within that time if you can replace Vikram, you can continue longer…"

Now, Mohit understood the complexity of the trap.

He was getting just 90 days. If he rejected this chance, he would be marked as 'refused onsite' and wouldn't be considered again. If he accepted, he would have to take on Vikram at onsite to keep his place. Failing to replace Vikram in 90 days, Mohit's onsite would end in a mere 3 months and post that he would not be considered for onsite for the next 2 years as he had travelled once. He wouldn't even be considered for promotion next year. Mohit was like a biker in Bangalore — caught between a chasing dog and a traffic cop waiting to extract some money from him. The westerners who are not familiar with the above 2 characters have also found another way to indicate such situations — i.e., he was between the devil and the deep sea. He silently deleted some of the offerings he made to the gods.

As a last resort, he asked Surya.

"Surya, can I not directly replace Vikram and you can ask him to look at the short project so that he will be forced to return in 3 months?"

Surya already becoming impatient with Mohit's long thought process responded.

"*Arre...yaar...* If you cannot take this simple challenge, how will you handle the customer ... how will you grow??"

Now, since this had become a basic question of his capability, Mohit decided to accept this offer.

He didn't know whether to be happy or sad about this.

All other customary practices of the onsite trip were completed. The treat prime of the project, Soumya, arranged an Amul joint treat. Most of the team members ordered the most expensive ice-creams and all the bachelors in the team packed sandwiches and drinks for their dinner as well. There was a separate dinner treat arranged for the managers in the star hotel nearby. Again, the most expensive food items and those that could not be tried at their own expenses were ordered. John and Rasool, who lost out the opportunity to Mohit, even brought their fat cousins for the treat. Mohit wanted to ask the fatties to get out, but for the sake of maintaining the 'nice guy' image in front of the girls, he backed out on that.

Finally the day of travel arrived…

Mohit's parents had arrived from his hometown to see him off. Not only that they had come, they had arrived with a set of items for him. Items included a big jar of mango pickle, utensils for cooking, etc. Mohit tried to explain to his mother that these were not required as he was going to California and there were lots of eating options. As any Indian mother, she burst into tears and Mohit was forced to pack them in also. She also handed over the cancelled ticket to Kashi as per his demand. She called Dhiraj's mother from the airport.

Mohit reached Bangalore International airport 3 hours before the flight time. This was his first international travel. He saw beautiful airhostesses walking with their cabin bags and hoped that at least few of them would end up in his flight. He reached the Singapore Airline counter for check-in. Since he didn't know how to pack, almost all his bags were having similar weight. The counter girl told he could not check-in like that and he had to first decide which was his cabin bag. Mohit was asked to go out of the line and re-pack. He had to pull all his stuff out. The smell of his pickle jar attracted a sniffer dog and it came running towards his bag. The bomb squad thought the dog had found a bomb. Imagining their prize money rewards, they rushed to the spot and took Mohit, his bags and the dog to the inquisition room. The next one hour he spent there and finally they came to know that it was just pickle. The dog was still not satisfied until it got a bit of pickle from the pack.

Because of the pickle-bomb fiasco, Mohit couldn't check-in earlier and he ended up getting a middle seat between two heavy-weight Indians. When his side of the plane lowered its height and the other side went up, he even thought it was because of the weight of those 2 guys. He heaved a sigh of relief when the 2 sides regained balance after a few seconds. Someone said, plane was taking a turn. If these fatties are in the flight, the plane may even overturn, Mohit thought. His lips silently uttered prayers. The fatties' snoring and frequent bathroom access disturbed Mohit's sleep. With lot of deprived sleep, Mohit arrived at San Francisco airport.

Mohit's pickle jar was attractive to US sniffer dogs also. The basic instincts of dogs are same, irrespective of whether they live in Bangalore BTM Second Stage or Napa Valley, California! The Californian dogs sniffed around his bags. US Customs caught hold of his bags and searched. They asked about his utensils inside the bag. One of the utensils inside the bag was the stick for making chapatti. The officers asked what it was used for. Mohit told it was for cooking. Officer got confused about what could be cooked in that stick. Finally Mohit had to mimic and show how it worked. All the officers stood around Mohit to watch the tamasha. Customs officer still didn't get convinced. Finally, Mohit left the stick and pickle jar with the customs officers.

Mohit crossed the immigration and entered the US soil without knowing what was in store for him.

Next day he reached office. Vikram didn't show any particular interest upon his arrival.

The next week was eventful.

Vikram not only did not help Mohit but also put a lot of blockers. He purposefully excluded Mohit from customer meetings. Mohit got firing from the customer for his absence. When Mohit asked Vikram about this, he told that he had sent the mail, but the mail didn't reach because the mailbox was full and the mail got dropped.

Outside office experiences were more eventful. After the first day, Mohit realized that it was not very easy to live in America without a car. From internet he had figured out the bus number to reach his office in Mountain View. The bus time was 8:00 AM. Like in India, he reached bus station by 8:10. By Indian standards bus would be delayed by 30 minutes at least. If it was in India, he would have reached only by 8:25 and even though the bus had left the bus stop, he would be able to catch the bus as it would have been stuck in the traffic block. But America was different, by the time he reached the bus stop, the bus had already left 10 minutes back. Then he had to wait for another 1 hour to get the next bus. In the evening, Mohit decided to take a cab. In India, we usually orally call cab's equivalent which is a rickshaw and then have a negotiation exercise and then start the journey. Mohit tried the same thing here but a few cab drivers told they would call the police and Mohit had to throw that idea away. The challenge was how to reach the hotel exactly. Mohit didn't know the address properly. In India, we can find the way by asking someone on the way. But, in America Mohit couldn't find anyone on the road, plus the driver was asking about some exit number. Mohit told some number and the driver took some road. After some 3 hours of driving and quite a lot of abuse from the driver, Mohit finally reached the place.

After the above commutation adventures, Mohit decided to rent a car and drive himself. He had bribed the Bangalore RTO office before leaving and had obtained his International Driving Permit (which looks like a ration card). He took the car out of the rental office and started driving on the left side of the road as he was used to in Bangalore. There were a few cars coming from the opposite direction which was usual in India so he didn't pay much attention. He even spat some abuses in Hindi to those opposite drivers for coming in the wrong direction. But, soon a police car standing nearby stopped him. Mohit didn't realize what it was for; he thought, like in India, the police was trying to get some money. In India Rs 100 is a good amount, he quickly calculated and flashed 2 dollars at the police, the US cops got surprised. Mohit thought the cops were asking for more, so he showed them $5. The cops thought Mohit was mentally sick and hence they let him go after giving him a warning.

The worst was towards the end of the week, when Mohit was about to leave for the weekend, a request got assigned to him. Customer manager had sent the mail asking for urgent solution by Monday. Mohit had seen Vikram spending time with the manager in the afternoon. He never thought such a bomb is in the waiting. On top of that, Vikram also sent a mail saying he needed update of the issue by Monday morning. To improve the marketing of the issue, Vikram had used all the required words like 'Hot issue', 'End customer critical', 'Critical blocker' etc., appropriately. Mohit had no other way but to burn his weekend for the issue. By Sunday, somehow, he fixed the issue and sent the details to Vikram.

On Monday morning when Mohit came to office, he saw some 10 mails on the same issue title in the mailbox. He thought the customer had already escalated the same. However, soon he realized that the mails were all appreciations for Vikram. Vikram had done the smartest thing in the world. He had taken Mohit's solution code and submitted the same and had claimed the credit for it. Mohit took a paper and wrote all the abuses he knew in the world to Vikram and dropped the paper in the shredder, as he was not confident of pasting it on Vikram's desk.

Similar kinds of smart moves kept on coming from Vikram and 2 months just flew like that. He had just 30 more days to outsmart Vikram and keep his place at onsite. The situation was like Indian cricket team batting on 45th over with more than 60 runs to win. Someone has to do a magical innings to get to the winning. Mohit had the least hope that he would survive. Without waiting for the last week, he started doing the shopping by going through his long shopping list. Already he carried a long list of shopping items as hard-copy which his parents had handed over to him when he left. On top of that, his sister sent mail every week demanding some or other items.

In the beginning, he thought he would buy the gifts from standard stores like Apple store, Nordstrom, Macy's, etc. Since his stay was going to be now only for 3 months and the onsite salary after the cuts of Infopro was just enough for living alone, he decided to change his target shops. With great difficulty, he found some dollar store nearby. The discovery of the dollar store relieved him as with only $50, he could get 50 items. He asked the shop keeper whether mobile phone was available there and the African-American shopkeeper gave a stern look. This prompted Mohit not to ask his next question — which was if he could get a TV from that shop.

Again some heavy wallet items were left which was impossible to purchase with Mohit's savings. Mohit sent a request to HR to approve some personal loan onsite. HR rejected the request the very next day itself saying that Infopro had stopped approving personal loans for people who had gone at least once onsite. Rather, the company was trying for a reverse loan from the employee since he was paid in dollars and the company was not doing very well.

It was almost towards the mid of June, there was one new enhancement which came in. It had to be completed by July first week. Most of the American employees didn't pick up that as all of them were looking forward towards July 4th summer long weekend and they didn't want to spoil their precious summer vacation. It is customary that such kind of enhancements will be reaching Indian engineers as guided missiles. Vikram never misses such show-off opportunities and he immediately picked it up in a project meeting. Customer manager was very elated and he sent an appreciation mail for Vikram for that also.

Mohit knew exactly what was going to happen. He knew that Vikram was not going to work on it as he had already booked his flights and hotel accommodation at Las Vegas for the long weekend. So, this had to reach Mohit only. As expected Vikram gave some reason and internally delegated the same to Mohit.

This was indeed a very critical feature for the customer. This was a new functionality which none of the competitors of the customer product had. Adding this feature and releasing just after summer vacation would give at least 3 to 6 months of lead time in the market. Hence the information regarding feature was very confidential and was strictly controlled.

As expected, during the long weekend, Vikram went away. Before leaving he had sent his usual mail instructing Mohit to send him the code once it was completed. Mohit completed the code. But this time, he decided to play the magical innings of risk. In the completed code, he made one small adjustment. In the help file which should display the support contact number, instead of the customer's support number, Mohit added the competitor's support number. As expected, Vikram came back from vacation and took the code and submitted the same without even reviewing the same.

The customer sent appreciation mail to Vikram again. Series of congratulations from Infopro management followed. All this time Mohit was smiling inside.

The product with the new feature went for beta sites. Since Mohit knew what was expected to happen, he made sure that he had the correct file ready and was always watchful on the issues reported. As expected, one night there was some support requirement. The beta person invoked the help of the product. The call landed in the support desk of the competitor.

Mohit was watching the issues and when the issue reported itself he knew what to do. He immediately submitted the correct file and fixed the problem that night itself.

The next day saw one of the biggest escalations Infopro had ever seen. The escalation said that the customer had never seen such an irresponsible engineer like Vikram who would submit the code with the competitor's contact number. The escalation went up to the CEO of Infopro. Vikram was immediately asked to pack his bags and return.

There was a separate mail which said that irrespective of the blunter of one Infoproite, another Infoproite had saved the day by immediately fixing the problem without further damages. The mail also said, Mohit was not familiar with the code, but still he had fixed the problem with record speed. Because of that reason alone the customer was refraining from suing Infopro or discontinuing the project.

The customer wanted Mohit to continue onsite long as the end customer support person. They also declared an award of 1000 USD for his timely and quick action. Mohit could buy most of his "heavy wallet" gift items with that. But, he could go home now only after a couple of years.

He gifted his $1 gifts to Vikram as he didn't get any time to buy gifts because he was asked to leave immediately.

11: Encounter with government — An un-usual value generation

If the sophistication of IT comes in contact with the lethargic nature of the classic Indian Government office, what will happen? It could change your life. No need to guess, just read this heroic story of another Infoproite.

On a monsoon day in June 2012, Manish was on his way to office. He was riding his bike through the Jail Road which connects the Sarjapur to Hosur Road in Bangalore. This is his usual route to Electronic City. There are more humps and potholes in this road and the percentage of tarred surface is less than 5%. After negotiating the mountainous humps and mine-like potholes, he reached the somewhat steady stretch near the Bosch office. As it had rained the previous day, the potholes were filled with water. Bangalore Corporation was considering connecting all the potholes to form a decent waterway between Sarjapur Road and Hosur Road which would be functional at least during the monsoons. Since there were humps at every 100 metres, the low lying area between 2 humps acted as a large reservoir. Manish even saw a water tanker pumping in water from the road to his tank, so that he could supply 'clean' water to one of the unfortunate apartment complexes nearby. Manish was already tired because of the 'mountain bike riding experience' in the morning and was getting late for the office. Suddenly, someone jumped in front of him. He thought someone jumped by mistake. Soon, he realized that it was not a "common man" but the Road Transport Inspector. It was almost end of the quarter and most likely he also would have some targets to meet.

RTO asked, "Hey, why your bike is not registered in Karnataka?"

Manish gave the standard answer, "Sir—I just brought it from my hometown last week."

The officer was not convinced. He had seen many such techies in the area who gave the same reason! Also, the officer had some personal grudge with techies as well. Manish later came to know that the officer once tried for engineering entrance exam and failed. From that day onwards he doesn't like engineers, especially IT people (who he believed are getting fat salaries for simply sitting in AC rooms and fiddling with the computer). So, he came up with the longest list of documents to be produced. He asked for driving license, RC book, Aadhar Card, Ration Card, etc.

While Manish was still fiddling with the documents, a piece of paper fell down from his hands. The officer picked it up and he had a glee on his face—like the one Sherlock Holmes may have had when he'd just cracked yet another great murder mystery. It was a petrol bill from Sarjapur Road pump, which was 2 months old... Manish cursed himself. I should have thrown it away much earlier.

Now the officer was in no mood to listen to Manish... Manish flashed a 50 Rs note. RTO looked at it uninterested. Then he flashed a 100 Rs note, RTO's face expression changed a bit but still was not positive enough. Manish wanted to flash two 100 Rs notes, but he had only one in his wallet! He wanted to ask if bribe is accepted through swiping machine. Looks like that facility is not yet available in Bangalore. They have only recently sent that recommendation to the department office. Since the negotiation stopped at 100 Rs and it was not going up, RTO acted as if he was a reincarnation of Harishchandra and shouted at Manish for trying to deceive an upright RTO with a silly 100 Rupee note. Then he went ahead with his 'Fine Collection procedure'.

He took all the documents and gave Manish a receipt...

Manish asked, "Sir where and how I can get the documents back...?"

The officer told — "In the afternoon at the RT office..."

That was the beginning of a complicated project. Manish still swears that this is one of the most complicated projects he had ever executed.

Since bike is an integral part of Bangalore life, Manish decided to venture into the RT office in the afternoon. Gayathri had promised for a Friday outing this week. Without bike, it would be impossible to do the same. Firstly, any other transport would eat up 2 hours of the total permitted 4 hours of outing time and secondly, because of the "closeness" you get from the bike ride.

Manish thought of finishing the work in 45 minutes including the to and fro commute. He reached RT office in the afternoon at 2:00 PM (in the process he fought with 2 Auto guys and finally got one Auto who agreed for meter charge but his meter was running faster than the auto wheel. In fact that meter was actually manufactured to be used in an airplane but by mistake it was fixed in this auto it seems).

At first, Manish thought it was a Government Holiday. No one was there at the seat. Later he realized that there were a few "Aam Admi" standing with dejected faces at different corners of the office. The lunch time displayed in the board was showing 12:30 to 1:30. Manish asked one of the "Aam Admi" standing there what had happened.

The 'Aam Admi' answered. "Sir … ithu Govermentu officuu..." (Literal Meaning—Sir this is a Government office, Actual Meaning—It is working as intended. Why are you asking such silly questions?)

After sometime Manish saw someone coming to one of the tables, he approached him and asked… "Sir, my papers…"

The tablewallah didn't lift his head even, Manish again asked, "Today morning my bike was caught by RTO, I want to get back my papers…" He finally raised his head and pointed his hand in one direction. There was another table there with no human being. In fact the table looked as if no human being had been using it for ages.

Manish waited near the table. He saw someone coming. The person who came didn't pay any attention to Manish. Instead, he went to the telephone and started conversing on that. After 10 minutes, he came back and looked at Manish. Manish repeated the question. He uttered the following words "The officer is on the field, papers have not yet come…" Now, unsure whether the papers were really there or not, Manish had no other option but to leave as he had to attend some meetings starting at 3:30 PM...

That was Manish's day one @ RT office.

Day 2 @ RT office:

One of Manish's friends dropped him there. He dreaded taking another auto which has the aircraft meter fixed in that. Already Manish was suffocating with the non-sophistication of the office. There was no AC, wherever you touch, there was enough dust to fill the lungs of an elephant, there was no computer, no big screens, and there were papers everywhere you looked. Plus, there was not even a good looking girl.

11:00 AM—No signs of any 'Babus' coming in. Manish was getting worried about his project meeting at 11:30. By 11:10, yesterday's Babu reached his table. After going for his tea and regular chit-chats he settled in his seat. By that time, Manish called his project manager "Shankar, I am sick today with dust allergy. Won't be able to make it to office today."

Manish went to the RTO Babu and asked about the papers. Though he met Manish yesterday, he didn't show any signs of that. Manish recited the whole story again and looked at the RTO Babu with hope. He looked through the file and confirmed that Manish's papers were there. Then Babu asked him to fill forms 45b, 77d and 88f and then return.

After searching around the building 5 times, Manish found that the forms were not available in the office but available in the Xerox shop outside. Looks like RTO has outsourced the same. Form says it is 'free', but it costs 10 Rs in the Xerox shop. You can very well assume that 4 Rs goes to the shop owner and remaining 6 goes to Babus.

Then came the next hurdle. Since the RTO office is at least 2 generations behind, the form has to be submitted as hardcopy. Like any techie, Manish had stopped carrying a pen since he started his career with Infopro. The only other option was to buy a pen as well from the shop. Knowing the techies well, the shop keeper already had a bundled deal if pen and form were bought together. Our petty shop keeper seemed to already understand the "Micro Economics" of bundling. But the surprise factor was that there was no discount for the bundle, instead he charged 1 Rs extra from MRP as the cost of the rubber band which was holding the 'bundle' together.

Manish said "I don't want the rubber band." But the shop keeper refused outright saying it comes with the 'bundle'. Manish realized that the shopkeeper knew many more things about 'bundling' than the professors in the IIM where he studied his MBA.

Post the form filling, Manish went back to the RTO Babu. RTO Babu was less punctual in only coming to office, but he was very punctual for his meals. In fact he was early for that part of his routine. He had left for lunch 15 minutes back…

As he had nothing else to do, Manish decided to have lunch. He walked into one of the 'Cyber Darshini' restaurants opposite. The restaurant had the 'standing mode' and 'sitting mode' of eating. Since Manish was standing the whole day, he decided to pick the 'sitting mode'. There was no one else in the sitting hall. The moment he sat down, a waiter came running and handed over the menu. The menu basically was a collection of all the North Indian and South Indian dishes so far invented since the time of Mughals. But, when Manish asked what was available, the waiter said,

"Sir… Only rice and chapatti."

It seems the menu represented all the dishes which were ever made in the restaurant plus the ones the cook is capable of making and even the ones the neighbouring restaurants can make, not necessarily what is actually there!!! Manish immediately noticed the similarity between the menu and proposal PPTs Infopro submits to the customers.

"How much time it will take?" Manish asked.

"Only 15 minutes Sir," the waiter answered.

Then the waiter went out of the restaurant through back door. Manish was curious where he was going. The waiter went straight to the roadside petty shop on the other side of the road and got rice and chapatti parcel.

"Another case of classic outsourcing." Again, he was able to draw parallel with what they do in Infopro "We claim that we have 2000 cloud engineers and the moment we get a requirement for 2 cloud people, we run to the contractors."

The waiter entered through the backdoor and he waited for 10 minutes to give a feel of 'preparing on order'. Then he brought the lunch. As the bill came, Manish noted that the 'pricing' included the charges for the sitting facility, cost of printing the menu, 30% margin for the restaurant, 20% margin for the roadside shop, 15% service charge, 2-3 Cesses and the cost of the leaf in which the meal was served.

'If I had gone to the roadside shop, I could have saved 80% of the bill amount.' Manish thought. 'I should never take my clients to this restaurant for dinner. Else they may get some new ideas and go directly to Infopro's contractors.'

"After all, there was a great deal of learning from this lunch." He tried to find the positive side. "Maybe this is what is called Lunch & Learn sessions."

@2:00 PM Manish was back… No sign of Babu yet.

@2:10 PM: RTO Babu is back post his lunch… Manish put the form in front of him as if placing the printout of proposal in front of customer. Mr RTO Babu threw the sheet back with a question "Where is RTOs attestation?"

@2:30 PM: After rigorous search, he found RTO's room. No Surprise, RTO was not at his seat…

@3:00 PM: No sign of RTO. The *chaukidar* in front of his room told, "Sir has gone for lunch to his home, will come back…"

@4:00 PM: No sign of RTO, but realized from a few other similar ill-fated people that for RTO to sign, a request in white paper is required. Manish had luckily not thrown the pen away. Managed to get white paper from the same shop. He had priced it at 6 Rs as there was no other shop around selling paper. This guy knows the demand-price curve very well. Manish suspected that this guy too must have done his MBA from a decent institute. He was executing the theories profitably. He could even take up the job of a visiting prof. in IIM.

Manish now wrote the request… (Realized that it's hard to write 5 lines without spell check and grammar check…)

@5:00 PM: Lost hope, left the place…

Day 3 @ RT Office

Experience is the best teacher. With two days experience, Manish kind of mastered the time slots when each Babu is available. He created a note in his smartphone as below.

RTO–Best chance to get 11:30 to 12:30. He calculated the probability as 60% during this time.

Payment counter–11:00 to 2:00 (As per the instruction board)

Clerks and Supervisors–11:00 to 12:00 and 2:30 to 5:30 (But rarely will be at their desks)

Manish decided to shoot for the best slot for RTO. He reached RT office at around 11:00. Luckily RTO was available. Manish stood in front of him like a Software Engineer in front of US immigration officer at Chennai consulate. RTO asked a few questions and finally signed the sheet.

Now, Manish ran to the tablewallah Babu where his papers were being held. No luck, Mr Babu had not reached yet. He had gone out for a short-smoking break — Just 40 minutes break, after which he came back. He searched for his spectacles for next 8 minutes. Once he found the specs, which was hung from his back collar, he took 4 minutes to clean it. After looking at the form for some time, Mr Babu told needs to assess the tax, to go and meet the Auditor. Manish made a mental remark, this moron should have told this before ... and BTW, when will the Government office learn to have something called check-list...

After an intense search, he was able to locate the empty chair of Auditor. After some enquiries, he found that the Auditor was on leave that day. (Don't understand these people, with effective working hours of only 3 or 4 hours per week, they need leave also in the middle of the week!). Manish made a mental note, when I retire from my own founded company after making crores of money and get into politics and become minister, I will surely introduce Individual Productivity measurement for these people. Since that was beyond moon distant dream and he was still in the middle of 2012, Manish had no other choice but to wind up the day.

Manish sent an SMS to Project Manager as below:

Not well, went to doc, WFH after 2:00

Day 4 @ RT office

The workflow resumed at 11:20 as the Auditor returned to office that day. When he realized that Manish needed the assessment, his face lit up. He put the ultimate weapon in front of him like a customer asking for hardware skill when we say we have all required software skills, "Where is the original bill?" He was least expecting that Manish would have the bill—the receipt given when he purchased the bike. Unfortunately for the Auditor, Manish had the original bill. With the disappointment of losing a prey, the Auditor assessed and arrived at the amount to be paid.

And thus the process entered the next phase.

@12:00 stands in the queue for payment

@12:30 reached the front of the queue. Waited for 5 minutes as the girl at the counter was busy chatting with her mother on mobile and asking about the lunch and also instructing her to take the clothes in from the outside as it was going to rain...

@12:35 realizes that there is another form called invoice form to be filled.

@12:50 manages to get the form and fill it (same method as the previous forms, outsourced to outside petty shop)

@1:15 reaches the front of the queue... Madam again on phone. Looks like Madam's mother had kept the *sambar* on the stove and gone to fetch the clothes. By the time she reached, the clothes got wet and by the time she returned back, the *sambar* got burned...

@1:17 Madam asked "How are you paying?" Manish pulled out his credit card, debit card and cash and says he is ready to pay by any of these means. Madam says the payment is possible only through DD... She is still angry that the *sambar* got burnt and the clothes got wet. Her voice is still quivering with anger and she was almost shouting at Manish as if he caused the *sambar* fiasco.

In short, there is no limit to surprises (again remembers about a check list)

@1:19 Manish jumps into an Auto and asks to go to the nearest ICICI Bank, Auto driver asks triple charge and then decided to offer a 33% discount and make it double charge. Manish asks the reason and auto driver says "Return *khaali* sir." Manish said "Me myself is the return..."

@1:25 Reaches ICICI.

@1:40 Comes out with DD...

@1:48 Reaches RTO office

@1:50 Stands at the tail of the queue again…

@2:00 PM madam shuts the counter door again and says closed for today. Come back tomorrow. Then she took her mobile and got into another argument with her mother at home — this time about some bills not paid.

@2:02 Manish came out and kicked a stone outside to vent his anger… Unfortunately, the stone hit the wheel of an autorickshaw parked by the side. The auto-wallah came out and caught him by the collar. He said the wheel is badly damaged and it can get punctured anytime now. Manish did not understand the logic, but had to shell out 200 Rupees to avoid any punctures in his body.

Then he sent the following SMS to his manager:

"Doc told to take complete rest, on leave today. Venky has already reviewed the HLD. I will catch up with him offline."

Day 5: Manish wakes up early and goes to the Krishna temple nearby. Offers prayers and offers additional goodies to Krishna if the work gets done today. He is still not confident. He goes to the nearby Ganesha temple and offers prayers.

Day 5@ RT office

Manish reaches RTO office, does the queue procedure and pays the fine and the tax and gets the receipt. Yesterday's drama gets repeated in parts, but the climax is different — work gets done. He then goes to the Table wallah Babu and asks for the paper. As told earlier, no lack of surprises. He couldn't find Manish's paper. After a rigorous search he finds it from the to-be-trashed bundle. Manish relieves his tension with a deep sigh and leaves the RTO office.

And Manish knows that the miracle happened only because of the blessings from Krishna and Ganesha together.

There ends Manish's epic in RT office.

As he takes an auto back to his home, and as the meter in the auto is speeding up like a rocket escaping earth's gravity, Manish's tired mind is now getting excited about thoughts of a new opportunity. The auto stops at his home, auto's meter stops 40 seconds later and Manish disembarks from the auto with a brightened face—he has decided his future professional career path. The 5 day's crash course in RT office has proved to be much more useful than the 3 years he spent in IT.

Cut to 2014! Manish doesn't ride bike any more. He has a chauffeur driven brand new Skoda Superb. He doesn't need to send SMS for leave, he himself is the boss. He is the CEO of a company called WeServe which he founded 2 years ago, the day after the 5-day crash course in RTO. The company does all the government related service through a web based portal. The portal contains checklists and instructions for each and every interaction with government. The Xerox shop wallah has become one of his territory managers. His agents go to the door step of the customers, deliver the forms and collect the signatures and money. The receipts are again delivered at the door steps.

The company is listed in the top 10 fast growing service companies by CNBC. Sequoia Capital had done 2 rounds of funding already. The company is awarded the most innovative Indian company of the year 2014. He attends entrepreneur seminars in Europe and US and takes classes in IIMs and IITs about his journey as an Entrepreneur. Pretty girls in these institutes surround him for Selfies. He obliges them as he respects women! When the guys approach for selfies, he tells them he is too busy to waste time away.

He has instituted a yearly scholarship for the best students among the wards of RTO employees. He says this is his way of thanking them for their motivation to take up his own path when he himself was not sure what to do with his life.

12: Bhikhari Shambhu Takes Over Infopro

Before becoming PM, Madhu was an excellent software engineer. After becoming PM, he became an 'Excel' engineer. His work involved creating, modifying and sending excel sheets.

When he is happy, he creates excel sheets! When he is upset, he creates some more excel sheets! When he got bored, he took some old excel sheets and changed the colour of the cells to cheer himself up.

He is a thin man, but he is now using only 'XL' size T Shirts!

To fast track his career, he had gone for executive MBA. When Madhu left for his MBA, he was a PM. As recession hit the B-School placements hard that year, he ended up coming back to Infopro in the same role. He wanted to get into a consulting firm so that he could at least regain part of the big money he spent on his MBA.

2 years after MBA, he was still waiting for an opportunity to use all the knowledge and MBA theories he learned.

Situation forced him to think about starting on his own. He formed a group of colleagues to discuss new start up ideas, but the ideas remained just the same—just ideas. Slowly the group became lean and people dropped off. He could not even get someone to accompany him to visit the 'Booze Paradise' on Friday nights.

It was another Friday. After finishing the excel sheets for the day, Madhu occupied the window seat at Booze Paradise in the evening — it was 9:00 PM. Through the window, he noticed the bearded beggar who was begging from each of the customers in front of the bar. He was ignoring the people who were going into the bar, but approaching everyone who walked out. And he was getting money from at least 40% of the people.

"Man...! His conversion rate is much more than a sales person in IT industry." Madhu got more interested. "He is applying some strategy for sure, that is why he is approaching only the drunken ones. Maybe an insight from his past experience. Or maybe he has done an MBA from a foreign university. He must have become a beggar because of the huge fees he paid to IIM."

As Madhu got out of the bar, the beggar approached him. He was wearing a torn, smelly kurta and pajama. His 'wardrobe' had not seen 'water' for at least 10 years. And he may not have taken a bath for 6 months at least. Lucky guy. His profession actually demands that he should not take bath and that he should look dirty. Madhu handed over a 20 Rupee note.

"Thank you sir." Beggar thanked him. Madhu was impressed by the beggar's politeness.

"*Arrey Bhai... Bahut paise mil rahen hain aap ko...*" Madhu initiated the conversation.

"No sir… just managing... Recession everywhere, Sir."

"*Arrey...* You can speak in English also..." Madhu was surprised.

"*Koncham koncham* … Sir. I was begging in front of Koramangala Forum Mall. You know — in that area, even cows and street dogs speak only in English. So, slowly I also learned."

"Great… *Kitna kamayenge ek din mein?*"

"Sir Monday to Thursday 2000 Rs. On Fridays, I make 3000 Rs Sir."

"Wow man, your hourly rate is more than the software engineer in my team." He was amazed.

"How much your income is increasing year on year?"

"Nothing much sir … just 5%."

"Lucky man … you are getting more pay hike than me." He said to himself. He did not want to reveal it in front of the beggar.

Madhu was completely floored. Till then, he had never thought about the economics of begging. A whole new window opened before him.

"Aap ka naam kya hai?"

"Shambhu, Sir. *Aur log mujhe Bhikhari Shambhu bulaate hain..."*

"Bhikhari Shambhu... Nice name."

This guy is making 2000+ a day without much effort. If he actually puts in some thought process and applies some real strategies, he can make much more than that. He can literally mint money. The management consultant in Madhu was slowly waking up. He had been looking for a consulting opportunity for last 2 years, and here was one, though he had to offer it for free.

"Shambhu… You know what … instead of your current daily collection of 2000, you should target 10,000. You should be ambitious. You can do it if you follow the right strategy." The alcohol within Madhu was moving his brain's 'spirit'.

"Mein kuch nahee kar sakta sir … mein savere nau baje se raat nau baje tak kaam karta hoon sir… yeh business *to* completely customer dependent sir… I can't control. It depends on the mood of the people to help."

Well, here is one guy who does not know much about the power of strategy. That is the best case scenario for a consultant!

Management consultants usually pounce on such guys and start lecturing them on the theories starting from Porter's 5 forces.

"See, whoever gives money to you, they are your customers. They are not giving money for free. You are actually selling them a hope—a hope that the God will keep an account of the money they donated and that the god will provide them with a pool-facing 4 BHK when they eventually reach the heaven after death."

That was news to Shambhu. In his long begging career, no one has given him such an insight.

Even Madhu was feeling very proud of what he just said. In fact he had rarely uttered such intelligent words in his life. He decided to keep a record of the brand of whiskey he had imbibed on that day. "Surely that whiskey is capable of simulating the brain, especially the management consulting portion of the brain!" he thought.

"So I'm not getting money for free, but I'm actually selling hope to the people!" Shambhu's eyes sparkled. He developed immense respect for Madhu, the management consultant, and was ready to listen to him and forget about other potential customers near the bar, to whom he could sell some hope and make money.

"Listen, Shambhu. Whichever industry you are in, you need to grow. You have every right to be ambitious about increasing your revenues," Madhu continued. Some of the words were his own; some others were prompted by the alcohol within him.

"You need to understand your customer. You need to follow a global delivery model."

"Sir... Global Delivery Model...? *Mujhe samajh me nahin aaya.*"

"Yes—GDM means, you have to be at the right place at the right time. You can't be at the same place all the time. Let me tell you — you should stand at this bar entrance from 7:00 PM to 11:00 PM. Go to the mosque gate on Fridays, wearing a skull cap. Go to church gates on Sundays; of course you should have a small cross on your neck. Go near the colleges during exam season. When the children give you money, raise your hand over their head as if you are blessing them. Go to the temple on Saturdays. When it is the season for Sabarimala pilgrimage, wear only black dhoti and kurta. Your conversion rate will be much higher."

"Also, you have to recruit good employees from Ethiopia, Somalia, etc., which are emerging markets and have a bigger talent pool than India for your industry."

"Sir great insights. While begging in E-City, many times I heard these words 'Global Delivery Model'. Now only I understood the real meaning. GDM means beg at the right place. Thank you so much sir."

Shambhu couldn't believe such insights were coming from someone outside the industry. "Sir one doubt .... Were you also in the begging industry before you started with IT career? You know so much about the strategies to be applied in the begging industry!"

"No... I started in the IT industry ... but sooner than later I may end up in your vertical. Not only me, all the project managers in IT industry will soon line up. Companies are planning to automate excel sheet manufacturing." Shambhu liked Madhu's frankness.

"Well, try the ideas I just shared. We will meet again next Friday evening. Tell me how it worked." Madhu said goodbye to his new friend. The past 20 minutes gave him a huge work satisfaction, he couldn't remember when he got it last time!

During the next week, Madhu manufactured more excel sheets, modified some and changed colours for some. He even deleted some excel sheets as they were not used for the past 5 years. When they were deleted, he felt like a part of his body was being severed off.

On Friday evening, Madhu went to Booze Paradise. As he parked his bike and got down, there he was—Shambhu, same dress, same stinking smell, but a wide smile on his face.

"Sir. Idea worked sir … good collection from temple and mosque." He paused and continued "I could not go to church, because I need to take at least the Sunday off."

Madhu felt jealous of Shambhu. He could take Sundays off! Madhu had to manufacture some 'critical' excels during most of the weekends.

Nonetheless, Madhu was happy. He had spent 20 lakhs to complete the MBA. For the first time, someone had benefited from those 20 lakhs. His business advice had worked for the beggar.

Madhu decided to start the next lesson based on the feedback. "See, when you are alone, you can't work on all the opportunities. You are just self-employed. That is why you missed out the church opportunity. You need to build a team. You must start employing people. You know begging industry is the largest unorganized sector in India. There is huge opportunity to build a large organization."

But Shambhu was not really convinced about building an organization. "Sir … you know, all beggars here are freelance beggars … they cannot limit themselves to working like a slave for an employer. I know in IT industry you can do that—but not in begging sir… Beggars value their freedom and self-pride more, especially the beggars in Bangalore."

"If you can't get employees from Bangalore, why don't you recruit from smaller towns? Look for tier 4 and tier 5 cities and villages. Find out the people who have lost their wealth in email fraud, in share market, or lost agriculture in drought, tsunami, floods, etc."

"Once you get people, you need to supply them with a 'bowl', 'stick' and 'appropriate clothes'. You need to work out some revenue-sharing arrangement with them."

"By the way, where will you accommodate them?" That was a genuine doubt from Madhu.

"No problem sir… *Yeh* elevated highway *hai na...*? From E-City to Madiwala … 9 kilometres long sir … no toll for sleeping under it!"

After the conversation, the beggar took a 100 Rs note from his dirty bag and gave it to Madhu.

Madhu was in 2 minds. For the first time, someone had paid for his management consulting. As per Indian culture, it is not good to refuse the first earning for a job. So he took 100 Rs from Shambhu.

Subi and Amit of his team had just reached BP on their bike and the first scene they saw was that of Madhu taking money from the beggar. They couldn't believe their eyes.

"Sir… *Aap ka* father *hai sir...*?" Amit looked at Madhu and Shambhu. "Both of you look similar."

Madhu was embarrassed. "Boss… I don't know him. I was just taking some change from him." But Amit was sure the transaction was only one-way. There was disbelief in his eyes. Madhu just wanted to somehow escape the scene. Instead of entering the bar, he left the place.

"It must be his father only…" Amit tried to explain the scene which they just saw. "Maybe Sudeesh and Manu already know about it. The other day they were telling that the 'PM beggar' has asked for the status again!"

"Yeah… must be… He does not want to share his 'Rags to Riches' story … that's all," Subi agreed.

During the next week, there was a rumour spreading in Infopro coffee rooms—that there is a PM in Infopro who is from very poor background. His father is a destitute.

When HR heard this, they thought of instituting a 'Rags to Riches' special award for the year or name it as 'Son of a Beggar' award. Later they scrapped the plan due to lack of budget.

Apart from that, the week passed off as a usual one. The IT project managers all over the world created, modified and deleted some excel sheets. Madhu also did the same.

Next Friday, Madhu reached BP a little late. He parked his bike a few metres away, checked the place to ensure his project mates were not there and walked towards BP. Shambhu was not there at his usual place in front of the bar.

"Must be on sick leave… Or is he working from home…?" Based on his IT mindset, that was the first thought which came to his mind.

He took his regular drinks from the bar and went home. After drinking, he thought about more ideas for improving Shambhu's business. He took a napkin and noted down all the points.

The next Friday when Madhu met Shambhu, he was happier than ever. He now had 5 employees begging for his firm at 5 different junctions of Bangalore. Last week, he had been to his village to recruit those people. He even started a bank account with the State Bank of Andaman and had deposited all the collections.

Madhu had started to get the kick. His strategies, whatever he learned in MBA, were working! That was an amazing feeling. He realized that the 20 minutes with Shambhu was giving him more work satisfaction than the long hours he spent with his colleagues in Infopro. So he was ready to start the next lesson.

"You should stop begging yourself. You should only supervise now. Your aim should be to improve productivity of each of the beggars."

Madhu continued. "You know—IT industry and begging industry are similar in many ways. Revenues in both cases are dependent on the number of employees. Your industry has beggars at the ground level. In IT industry, these beggars sit at every level. In both cases, people management and motivating them for high productivity is important."

"You need to have an HR person to devise policies and track productivity improvements of your people. Recruit someone from IT as both industries are similar."

"But Sir, will someone leave IT and join my company?"

"Of course. Why not? You don't know the guys in IT. You just need to offer 50 paise more than what they get now. They will join for sure. Also, the other thing they look for is 'better' position. If he is a consultant, take him as a senior consultant. If he is a sweeper, just take him as a senior sweeper. They will join the next day."

"Is that right ... sir...? I thought these IT people are ... you know, very sophisticated and complex people," Shambhu told frankly.

"Darwin did not mention it in his Theory of Evolution—but actually these IT people are the simplest of the mammals. If you offer grass and water to a cow, it will come with you. Similarly, just offer 50 paise more and a 'senior' role to an IT guy ... he will join you... It is so simple."

"Is it...?" Shambhu was enlightened to the core. The image of an IT engineer completely changed in his mind.

"Remember, these beggars are your biggest asset. You should know that every morning, the biggest assets of your company walk out of their hut to the different junctions of Bangalore. They should be treated well."

"Next week onwards, you can come to my PG and we can meet there. I don't want to discuss important business matters in an open area like this." Madhu gave him his PG address.

Next weekend, Shambhu came to Madhu's PG.

"Sir I have decided to name my company 'The Bowl' (TB). Our symbol will be an earthen begging bowl. A lamp will burn on the bowl — a lamp of hope. How is it sir...?"

"Very good. It captures the very essence of the company. Decided on the tagline?"

"Yes sir... *Yeh Bheekh Mange More.*"

"...Hmm... it lacks the punch ... not seductive." Madhu got into proposal review mode.

"What about — Beg your way to success...?"

"Not very appealing." Madhu shot down that too.

"Then what about this Sir — Powered by a 'bowl' and driven by a 'stick'?"

Madhu thought for a second and replied "Leave it for now ... you may get into some IP issues."

"Ok — then what about — Gods own people?"

"Yeah ... that sounds good..." Madhu was in complete agreement "You know what! There are even states in India which invoked god's name like this when they were not able to bring about any development themselves. That strategy worked."

"Besides, this tagline stresses the fact that you are actually in the spirituality industry. Anyone who gives money to 'The Bowl', is actually making an EMI payment towards his pool-facing 4 BHK in heaven."

So, one important part of the discussion was closed.

"Ok let's get into operations discussion..." Madhu continued. "How is your employee strength and revenue as of now?"

"We have good growth rate sir ... we have now 64 employees. In fact, we have more opportunities than our employees can cover ... even freelancers have started joining us sir ... they see that we are treating our employees well."

Then he paused for a minute and reluctantly asked "Sir ... when would you join us Sir...?"

Madhu was about to reply, but at that moment someone knocked at the door.

Madhu opened the door. It was Subi and Amit. They had come to invite him for Amit's sister's marriage. Amit did not know Madhu's PG so he took Subi along. They saw the same Bhikhari sitting on Madhu's bed inside the room. The same Bhikhari who gave money to Madhu was on his bed now!

"Please come for the marriage sir... Sorry for disturbing..." Amit and Subi left.

"Did you see that...?" Amit spoke while both of them walked down the stairs from first floor of the PG. He had a shock-filled expression on his face.

"What?"

"I don't think that Bhikhari is his father. But they have some other relationship."

"See, last week, Madhu took money from the Bhikhari — we saw that. And today, the Bhikhari is in his bed. You are getting the connection?"

Subi also got the shock of his lifetime.

"Maan...! When he said he had to look for other sources of income, I did not know he would do these kinds of things."

"Should we report to HR?"

"No, it is matter of personal preference and choice. That is what Martina Navratilova says. These kinds of relations are allowed in western countries you know." They walked away to the bike parked in the adjacent street.

The next week, there was another rumour doing the rounds in coffee rooms of Infopro. Many people from other departments also came to visit their friends in Madhu's project, so that they could see the central character of the rumours.

Some of his junior team members cancelled the one-on-one meeting they had planned with Madhu. They did not give any reason.

2 days later, he got a call from one Mr Reddy asking if he would be joining the next weeks LGBT meet up in Bangalore. He even offered Madhu to take up the organization's area head position in E-City. Madhu thought it was a career consulting company and asked him to send the JD. He also said he was ready to join if he was offered a 'Senior Area Head' position. He heard some murmurs and internal discussions from other side of the phone. Mr Reddy finally said "We will see if we can create that post. Will call you back."

At the moment, he was not very keen on a job change, his mind was fully occupied with his management consulting assignment working big time for The Bowl (TB).

TB was growing by the day. Shambhu could not handle the growth himself. He had to conduct interviews, conduct induction sessions, handle payments to the employees, etc. He wanted additional help. Shambhu had recruited one HR person from an IT company to help him in recruitment and induction. But he did not finally join, because another competing IT firm offered 75 paise compared to the 50 paise hike offered by Shambhu.

Madhu gave him the contact number of the contract employee supplier which Infopro was using to get additional java resources.

The contractor was sceptical initially, but he agreed after he heard the payment terms from Shambhu. Java skills were not selling like before. So, this was an alternate revenue source for sure. So, he provided some resources to Shambhu to manage HR, recruitment, PR and brand building functions.

Shambhu's company had grown to 300 employees in just 5 months. He called a meeting of all senior employees on the Government School ground on Hosur Road on Sunday, for discussing the strategies.

Shambhu, the chairman, gave the keynote speech. "We are one of the best employers in this sector. Our growth rate is more than many of the leading corporations of the world. Many IT people who lost their jobs also have submitted their resumes in our portal 'bhikari.com". We will do proper scrutiny and recruit only 10% of those people who have high BQ—Begging Quotient."

"The newly recruited people have asked to create a social networking platform for all our people. There are 2 guys from IT who joined us last week from a social networking company linkedin.com. They will set up the networking site for us 'BeggedIn.com'. They will train all of us on how to use it. Through that medium, we can interact with our fellows in other countries too and learn a thing or two from them regarding how they improve revenues."

"This Diwali, we are giving 20% hike for the best performers. Minimum hike will be 14%. We will make this a world class corporation."

All beggars clapped and rejoiced. *"Ab hamare liye Ache Din aanewale hain"* they said in chorus.

It was already 9 months into Madhu's consulting career. TB continued the high growth rate. The number of its employees is in thousands now. Chairman Shambhu and consultant Madhu got into one of the conference rooms in Crowne Plaza Hotel — completely paid for by Shambhu. He has started shaving daily and he wears suits and ties. He roams around in Bangalore in a brand new Benz car — chauffeur driven!

"Sir, we are getting very good revenues sir… The 'temple' vertical and 'mosque' vertical are doing very good. In 'church' vertical, we need to increase the man power. Since it is Sunday, people are not willing to go. I am now offering Overtime charges."

"The transport vertical is facing some pricing pressures, Sir. Our guys in bus stand and railway stations are not getting much. People are not giving because the ticket price has increased. You understand no, Sir? It is about the reduction in disposable income due to increased ticket price. That is why I said pricing pressure."

"By the way Sir, I am even considering giving a promotion to the vertical heads as presidents."

"Good, you need to groom your future CEOs." Madhu supported that move. "It is not only the founders who can become CEOs."

"We are also opening our training centre in Hosur Sir... We have named it '*Bhiksha Ki Shiksha*'.

"Great... Education is the cornerstone in any people-based industry," Madhu agreed.

"Another thing — You need to quickly implement IT for your company. Assign someone to analyze the IT needs of the firm."

"Ok Sir... I will put my IT folks on that activity Sir. There are quite a few IT folks in TB now. They lost their jobs in IT, don't have any other skill, so joined TB as freshers. They are picking up fast, with minimum training Sir... I am amazed by their learnability. I think IT people are best suited for this job Sir..."

"Now we need to find some venture where we can invest all the money we got," Shambhu raised the next agenda item in his list.

"Well, you can be an angel investor. There are many entrepreneurs in Koramangala area who are looking for VC funding. Every other building has a start-up in it. You just go to Koramangala 7th Sector and ask the first guy you meet — whether he is looking for a VC fund, the answer will be yes 50% of the time. If he says no, he must be a visitor to Koramangala."

"Will do Sir. At least now you should consider joining us Sir," Shambhu insisted. Madhu still could not take a decision. He was waiting for the 'right' moment.

"You should now expand your operations to other countries as well. Open a centre in the US, your revenues will be in dollars. But keep one thing in mind. You must recruit US employees locally. Don't give your Indian employees onsite opportunities. Later, they will take it as their right to go onsite and will start fighting for it. You should learn from other similar industries."

"True, I agree. We must expand operations. And don't give onsite opportunity for the *desi* folks. Got it sir." Shambhu was convinced.

"One more important thing—You should target non-linear growth. If the revenue remains proportional to the number of beggars employed, it will affect your growth rate going forward. Need to find ways to initiate the next version of TB. You can call it TB+ or TB 2.0 and the focus need to be on non-linear growth."

The discussions and consulting advices went on till late night.

In the next 6 months, Shambhu and his TB made a series of investments in 6 start-ups. 5 of them were not doing good, but the 6th one— 'Mopps' which was developing mobile apps— went big. The 'Mopps' catapulted Shambhu into the next orbit.

In Infopro, life progressed as usual. Madhu did not get a promotion as there was no vacancy in his vertical. He was asked to go to Rwanda Development Centre as there was a vacancy for senior PM. There were 2 SPMs, one of who got killed last week in the civil war. The other guy was in ICU. Madhu could replace anyone of them (he had a choice). Madhu decided to stay back in Bangalore. He said Rwanda's climate wouldn't be good for him.

He had been pleading with his GM for an onsite assignment for the past 3 years, and he got it now. He left for Canada for 6 months.

As the chief advisor left, Shambhu's VPs found a consulting company to work with TB for their future investment advice.

The first thing the new consultant did was to find fault with everything the previous advisor had done. They said the previous advisor, i.e., Madhu, was actually taking the company for a ride. TB has a much bigger potential but Madhu misled them on each of the important decisions.

Then they made a 300 slide presentation on how TB can outpace its growth rate in next 1 to 3 years. Shambhu slept through slide 2 to 98. On slide 99, consultant wrapped up the presentation, as he was not able to hear his own voice because of the loud snoring of Shambhu.

New consultant also got 4 articles published in Business newspapers about Shambhu and his vision for India's downtrodden. They even got him a TV interview. Shambhu was hugely impressed with that. He felt terrible about the time he wasted with Madhu, the incompetent, unprofessional consultant (as the new consultant firm described him).

With success of Mopps, Shambhu was now a dollar millionaire. His new consultant presented to him new potential investment opportunities every day.

"Sir, next week, there is an invite from IIM to take a session on Entrepreneurship. Should we accept the invite, Sir?" Consultant asked Shambhu.

"No, I don't have time next week, I need to take some break. Book my ticket to Phuket. Tell them I have time only next year."

"Thank you sir. Will do."

Then the consultant started giving ideas about investments.

"Sir, what about buying an IPL team sir…? That is the fashion among millionaires now. In our research, we found that one of the IPL teams may be available soon, as the owner is losing his aeroplanes, bungalows, his bulgan beard and even his *chaddhis* sir."

"Don't say *chaddhi*, speak like a professional, say 'underwear' instead." The consultant's manager, who was in the meeting, intervened. In fact that was the only input from him in the entire meeting. Managers are same everywhere!

"Sure Sir." The consultant agreed with his manager and turned to Shambhu again.

When Shambhu showed some interest, the consultant opened up a 320 slide deck and started a presentation on IPL.

When the consultant was jumping to the 8th slide, Shambhu fell into deep sleep. Consultant stopped at slide 87, due to snoring.

Shambhu's phone and emails were now being managed by the consultants, so Madhu could not reach him for a catch up. Even otherwise, the new consultants ensured that Shambhu had no love left for Madhu now.

Meanwhile, Infopro was looking to selling its 30% stake as one of the JV partners wanted to exit. Infopro's CFO was a friend of Shambhu's consulting company CEO. Both of them together took Shambhu to Bangkok and by the time they returned, Shambhu was the owner of 30% stake in Infopro.

There was a news conference organized—Shambhu and his team answered the scribe's questions.

"What led you to pick up stake in IT industry Sir?" One scribe asked.

"Well, all of you know about 'The Bowl' and my original industry. In the current macro environment, begging industry is definitely a high margin business whereas for IT, the profits are dwindling. But, you know, there are a lot of similarities between the 2 industries and we expect to draw a lot of synergy between the 2 companies."

"Look at it—both the companies' revenue depend on the number of people, both of us follow a dress code, there are too many skilled people in India who are eligible to get into both industries."

"The Bowl is going to start using IT soon, and I hear from my friends that there is a lot of begging happening in IT companies—for onsite, for promotion and for salary hikes—that gives a skill match and cross dependency even."

"We will cross-train our employees in both firms and share the best practices between the two. For example, half yearly appraisals in Infopro—we have already adapted the same in TB and called it Begpraisal."

"Going forward, we will see if we can share the transport facility between the 2 companies. Also planning to have job rotation between the 2 firms at the project manager level and above."

The business news channels ran a day long story and discussions on the synergies between Infopro and The Bowl.

By the time Madhu was back from onsite, Shambhu was operating out of the Inofpro HQ building, as the Board member.

Madhu tried to get an appointment with Shambhu. Shambhu's consulting partner refused to give an appointment. He said the Director meets only VP and above. When Madhu said he was Shambhu's friend, the consultant laughed it off.

Next Monday, after lunch, the HR Manager and GM Ramesh Srinivasan called Madhu.

"Madhu, you know what—the new director and his team have taken up the task of rationalizing the employee strength. You know his team is from one of the top 4 global consulting firms. They have decided to remove redundancy at the Project

Manager level…"

"…I am afraid we will have to allow you to find another job." Madhu got the shock of his lifetime.

At 6:00 PM, he got all his papers and he rode his bike straight to Booze Paradise. He wanted to take as much 'medicine' as possible to bring down the mental tension.

Same bar, same window seat.

"Maan…! I should have joined TB when Shambhu asked me to. Had I done that, I would have been in the director board of Infopro now! And I could have kicked out this Ramesh Srinivasan and that HR guy who fired me."

Madhu did not know what to do. "Maybe I can join TB as a fresher."

He looked at the corner where Shambhu used to stand. That position was empty now! A huge 500 watt bulb flashed in his mind. "Wow, there is an open position, which has a huge growth potential."

'The Bowl' has the monopoly in Indian Begging Market. What about creating a world class competitor? For now, I can recruit one guy to start his 'work' in front of BP.

Right then, his phone bell rang. It was Mr Reddy from LGBT.

"Mr Madhu, we considered your request. We have decided to give you the post of Senior Area Head – E-City in our organization."

Madhu's happiness had no boundaries. I may have lost my job, but I have already got 2, not one, open positions to fill in!

"I must check in Wikipedia which are the main products of this company LGBT." He had not checked Wikipedia yet to find out about LGBT.

"I will work in LGBT during daytime and spend time on my own business in the evenings. Lucky me."

Madhu finished his drinks. With a new vigour and determination, and with dozens of MBA theories and hundreds of 2 by 2 matrices up his sleeve, he walked out of Booze Paradise, to conquer his new future.

The Glossary

No book completes without a glossary. We present you an IT glossary with our definition for the terms used in this book:

	Actual expansion	**Our definition**
HRD	Human Resource Department	The department which reminds every IT employee that he/she is just a resource — like the computer in the cubicle, table in the meeting room or the cleaning brush in the toilet.
PM	Project Manager	Rather should be named as "Punching Bag Manager" as he gets punches from all directions — boss, reportees and peers.
PPT	Power Point	Contrary to the name, its contents end up as powerless and pointless. In any slide deck, 49% come from past decks created by someone else and 49% comes from Google. First slide and 'Thank You' slide are created by the 'owner' of the deck.
RFP	Request For Proposal	Customer asks for what they want through RFPs. Vendors give responses with what they have, which often addresses 5% of what is asked. Subsequent phases of RFP involve convincing the customer that they really need only that 5%.
DM	Delivery Manager	Who is unsure about what gets delivered under him. In most cases, the only delivery he is aware of is the pizza delivery which he orders whenever his wife refuses to cook for him.

GM	General Manager	He is 'generally' considered a manager, though he does not manage anything 'in general'.
CEO	Chief Executive Officer	Legend says, the buck stops at his office. We had never seen any buck walking to his building till now.
ESAT	Employee SATisfaction	An imaginary concept which no one in IT industry had seen or felt yet. Only HR department folks claim that they can measure it.
HLD	High Level Design	The document which gives the impression that there is always a low level design to follow.
LLD	Low Level Design	The document which will have no resemblance to the actual design which will be implemented or the high-level design which preceded.
KM	Knowledge Management	Those who usually talk about knowledge management have no knowledge of any sort of management.
CCD	Café Coffee Day	A place which works as substitute for Bar inside the IT campus where romance, frustration and depression gets vented out.
CMMI	Capability Maturity Model Integration	The "something" whose abbreviation, expansion, implementation and result have no connection with each other.
BA	Business Analyst	He does reverse engineering of the features of a software product and presents to the customer as business requirements. Many a times customer falls for it.
TL	Technical Lead	He is 50% developer, 50% manager. But ends up doing 100% of both. Team members consider him responsible for all their salary/workload woes. PM considers him responsible for all the project delays and bugs.